W9-AIA-478

Math
Skills

Grade 1

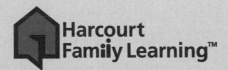

Harcourt Family Learning™

© 2004 by Flash Kids
Adapted from *Steck-Vaughn Working with Numbers, Level A*
© 2001 by Harcourt Achieve
Licensed under special arrangement with Harcourt Achieve.

Illustrator: David J. Brooks

Harcourt Family Learning and Design is a trademark of Harcourt, Inc.
All rights reserved. No part of this publication may be reproduced,
stored in a retrieval system, or transmitted, in any form or by any means,
electronic, mechanical, photocopying, recording, or otherwise,
without prior written permission from the publisher.

ISBN: 978-1-4114-0106-8

Please submit all inquiries to FlashKids@bn.com

Printed and bound in Canada

Lot #:

26 28 29 27

01/14

Flash Kids
A Division of Barnes & Noble
122 Fifth Avenue
New York, NY 10011

Dear Parent,

You've taken the first step toward your child's success by purchasing this book and making time to work with your child. Using *Math Skills* as a learning tool will make that time effective. This book contains fun illustrations and activities to keep your young learner entertained. In addition, *Math Skills* includes materials required by both state and national standards. If your child is learning it in school, this book covers it.

Starting with basics like counting, addition and subtraction, your child will learn all the facts necessary to understanding first-grade math. In this book you'll also find sections on place value and number sense, money, telling time, and geometry and measurement. Throughout each unit, your child will be given ample opportunity to estimate, compare, find patterns and use logic. Exercises like these help your child develop important thinking and problem-solving skills. These areas of knowledge are the foundation upon which your child will build more complex math skills.

One of the most difficult things about math is the potential frustration it poses for some young learners. *Math Skills* counteracts this problem by providing examples on almost every page. The harder topics are covered from many different angles, to ensure that your child can move forward snag-free, without giving up. In addition, the answer key at the back of the book can act as a reference for you and your child.

As you and your child work through the book, try to show your child how to apply new skills to everyday situations. For example, have your child estimate how many glasses of juice can be poured from a carton, or how many pieces of dollar candy can be purchased with a five-dollar bill. As your child draws connections between concepts presented separately in this workbook, he or she learns to reason mathematically, an ability critical for success through future years of math instruction.

Also, consider how you can turn the following activities into fun math exercises for you and your child to do together:

- Counting, adding or subtracting simple household objects, such as toy blocks or buttons;

- Estimating how much time is left before the next planned activity of the day;

- Determining the proper number of coins needed to buy different items at the grocery store;

- Using a calendar to count how many days until an important event such as a birthday, holiday, or school vacation;

- Making graphs to organize information, such as household chores or school progress;

- Identifying and counting the plane and solid figures spotted during a car trip or walk around your neighborhood.

Use your imagination. With help from you and this workbook, your child is well on the way to math success!

table of contents

unit 1

unit 2

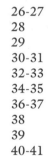

unit 3

unit 4

Place Value and Number Sense

unit 5

Money

unit 6

Time

unit 7

Geometry and Measurement

Counting to 5

Draw a line from each number to the matching group of objects.

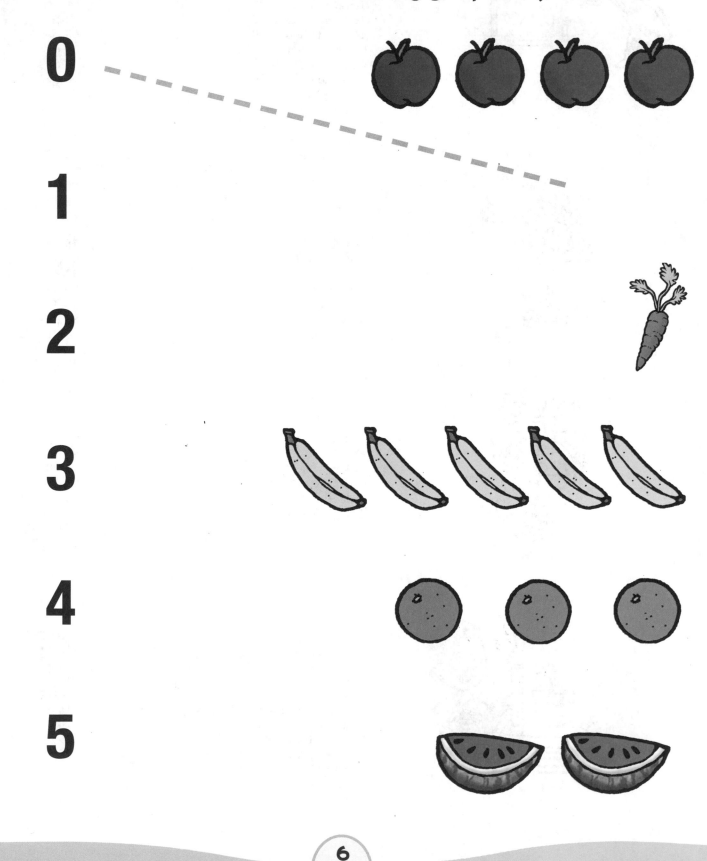

0

1

2

3

4

5

Counting to 5

Color a group of apples to match each number.

2

5

0

3

1

4

Counting and Numbering to 5

Count the number of candies in each group. Write the number.

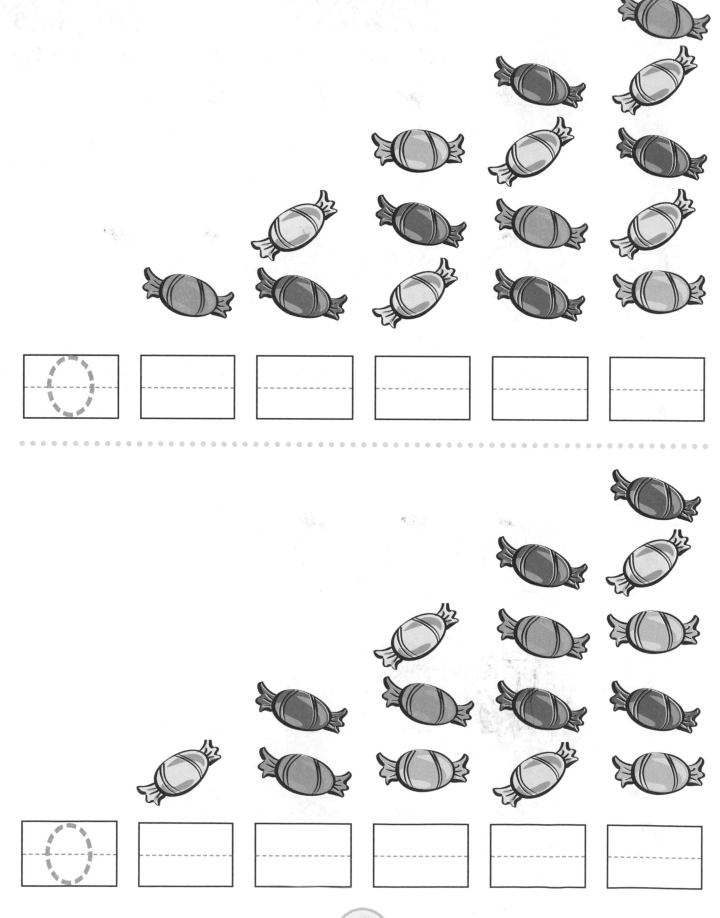

Count the number of candies in each group. Write the number.

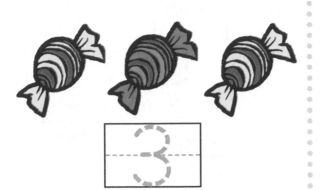

3

_____

_____

_____

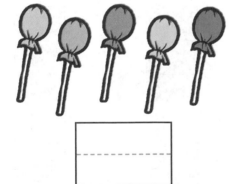

_____

_____

Counting and Numbering to 10

Count the cubes in each group. Write the number.

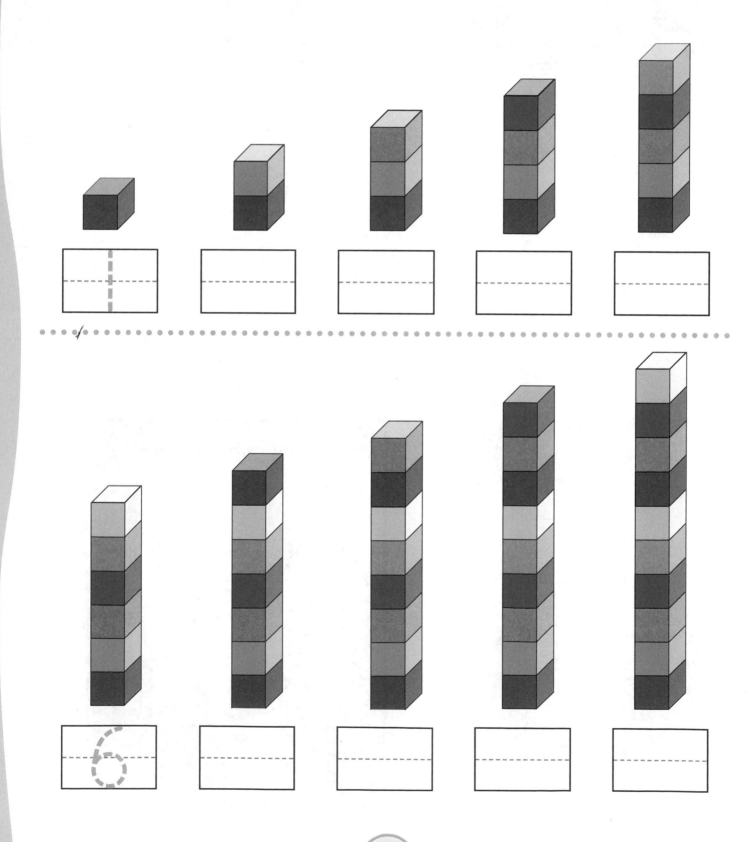

Count the cubes in each group. Write the number.

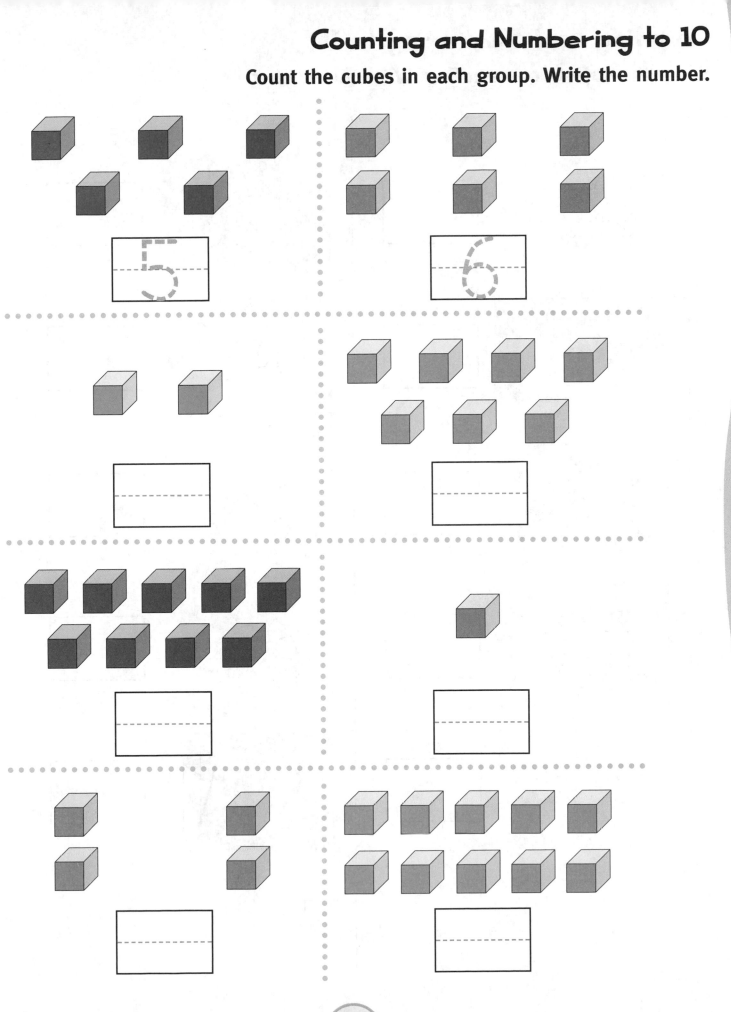

Counting and Numbering to 10

Count the objects on each flag. Write the number.

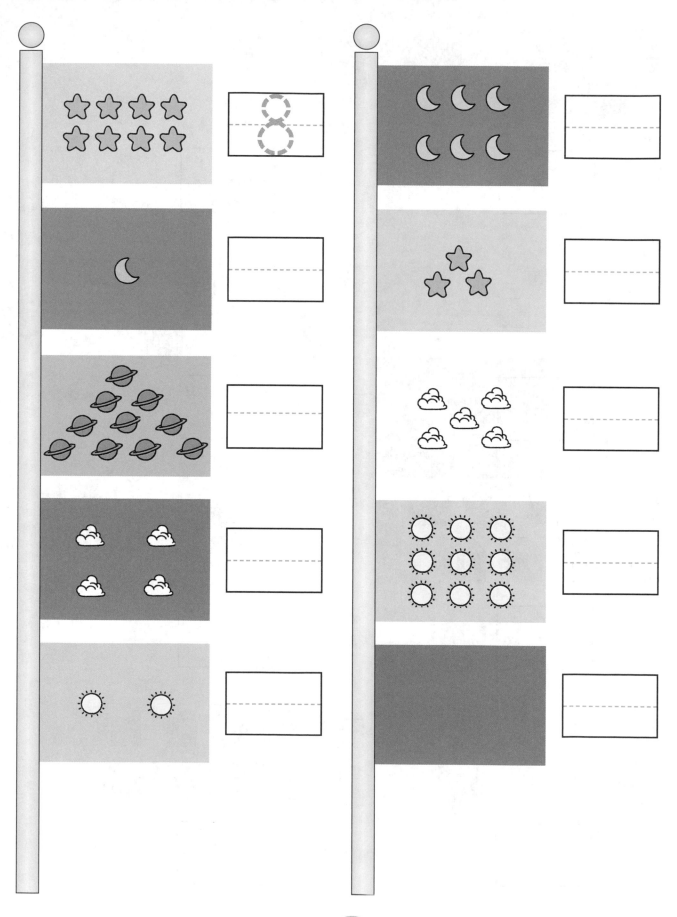

Counting and Numbering to 10

Write the numbers 1 to 10 in order.
Draw a line from each number to the matching group of objects.

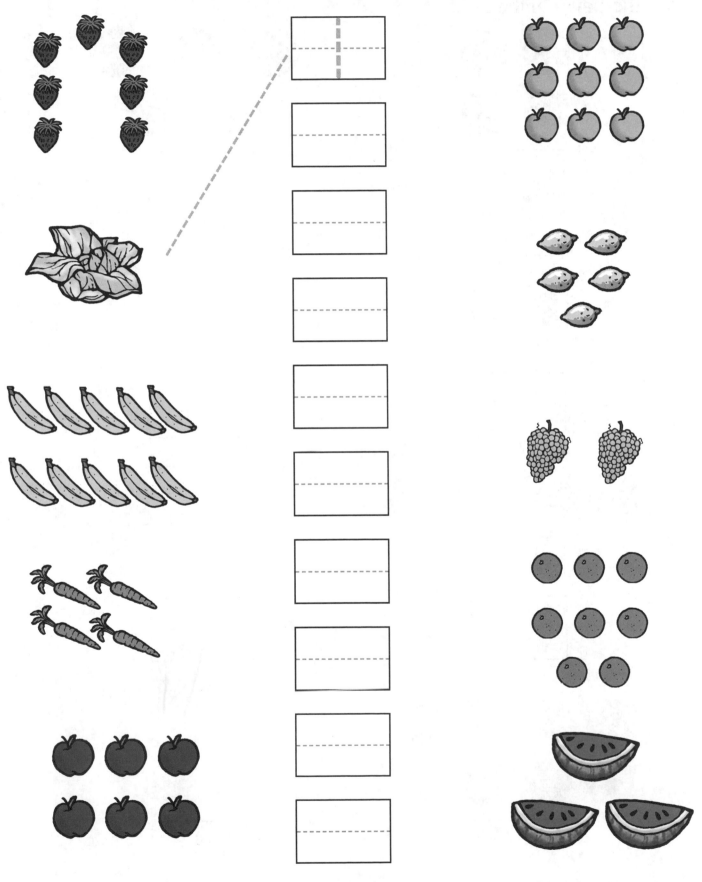

One More

Count each group of circles. Write the number.
Next to each group, draw a group with one more circle.
Write the new number.

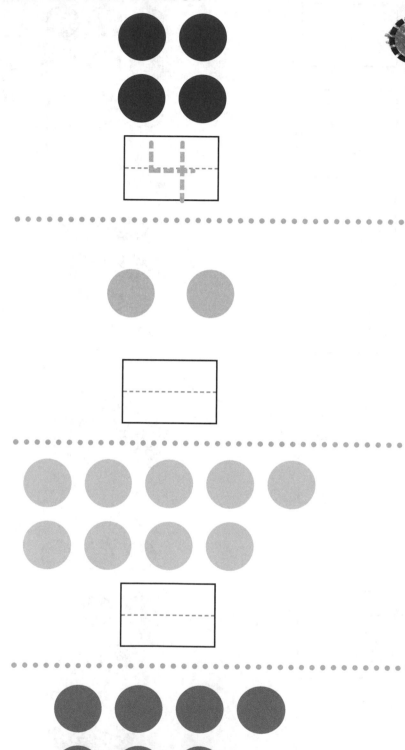

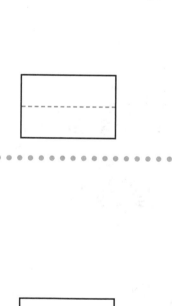

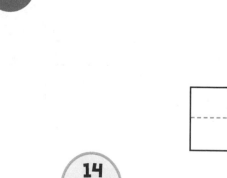

One Fewer

Count each group of circles. Write the number.
Next to each group, draw a group with one fewer circle.
Write the new number.

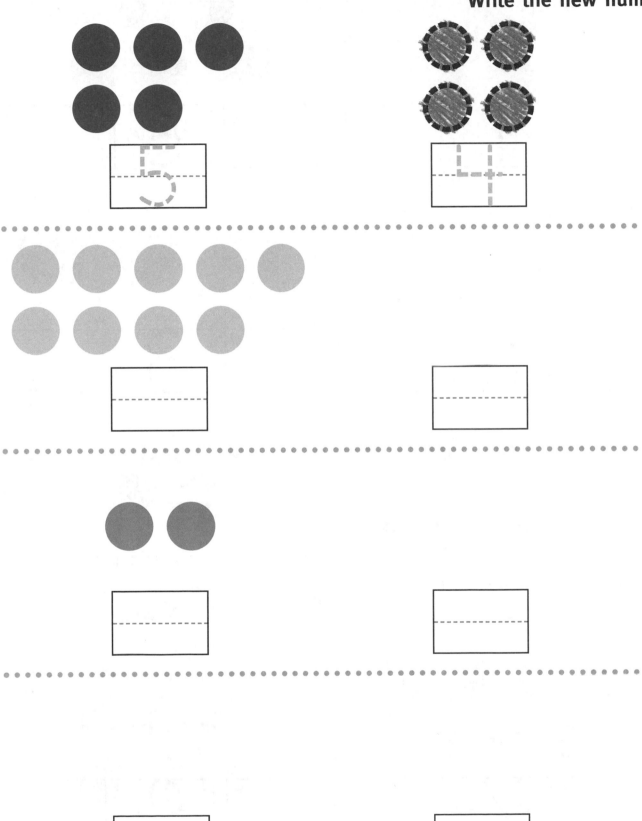

Before and After

Write the numbers that come before and after the ones shown.

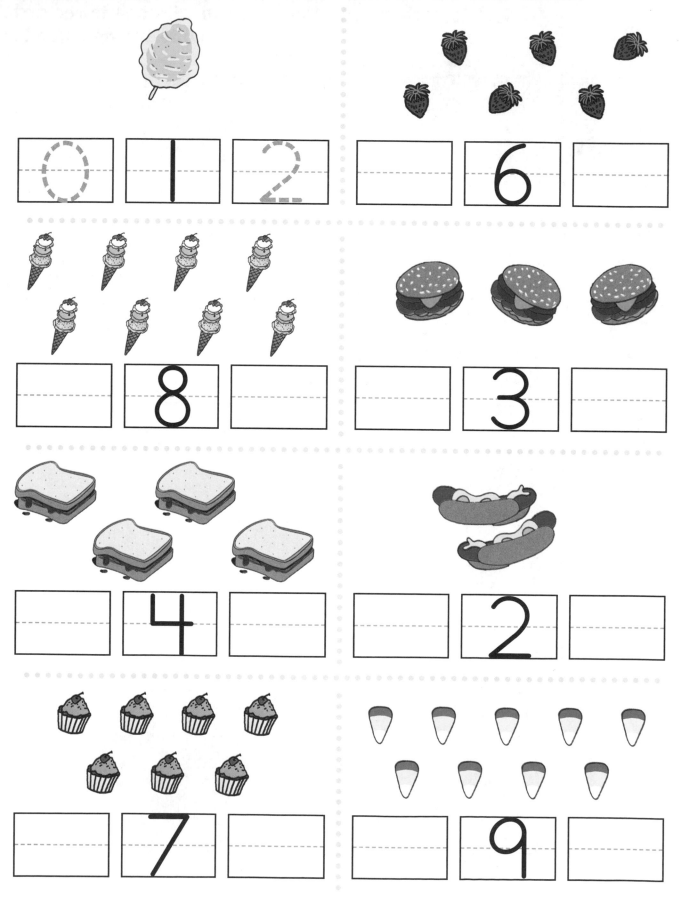

Missing Numbers

Count the windows in order. Write the missing numbers.

Missing Numbers

Write the missing numbers in the train cars.

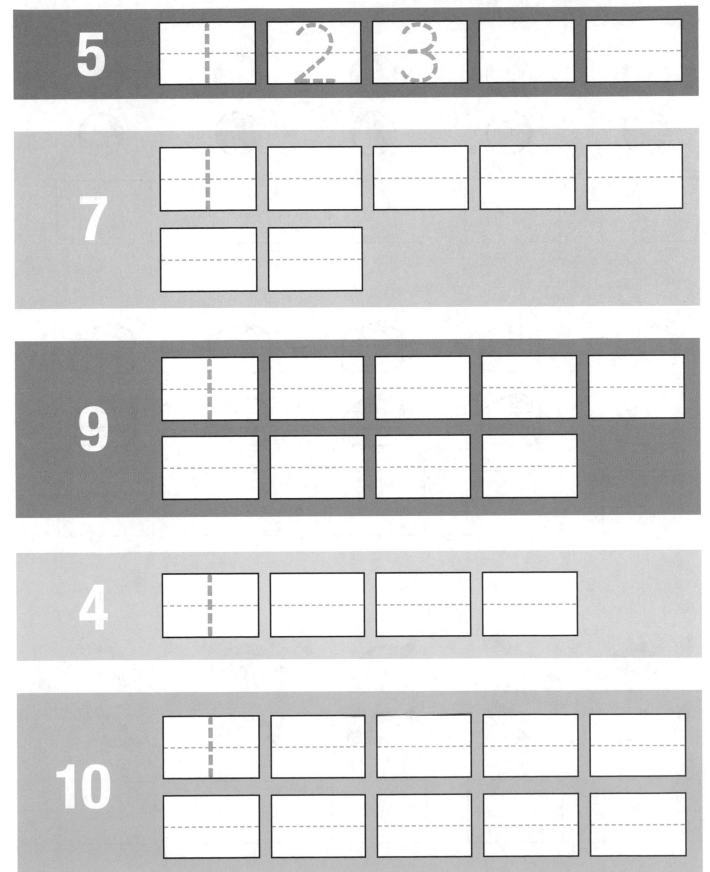

Skip Counting

Skip count by twos. Write the numbers to show how many in all.

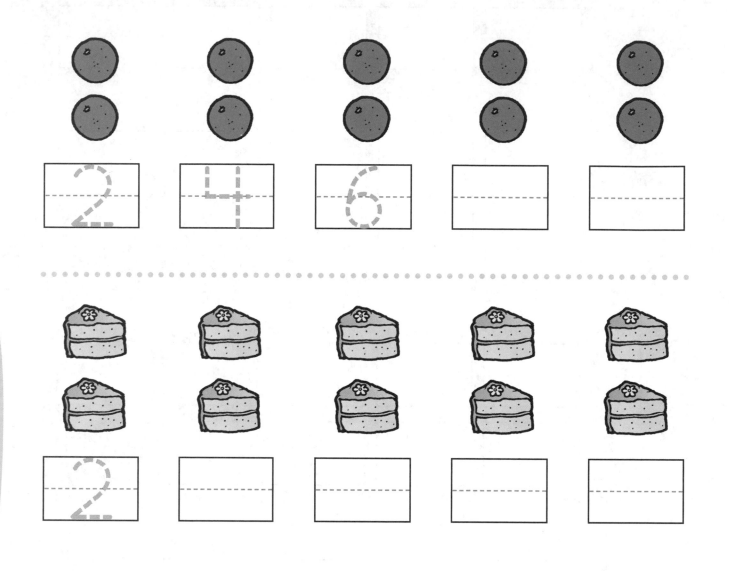

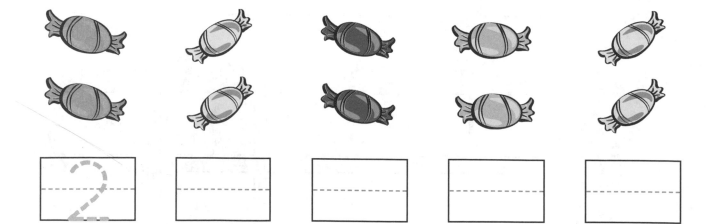

Skip count by twos. Write the numbers to show how many in all.

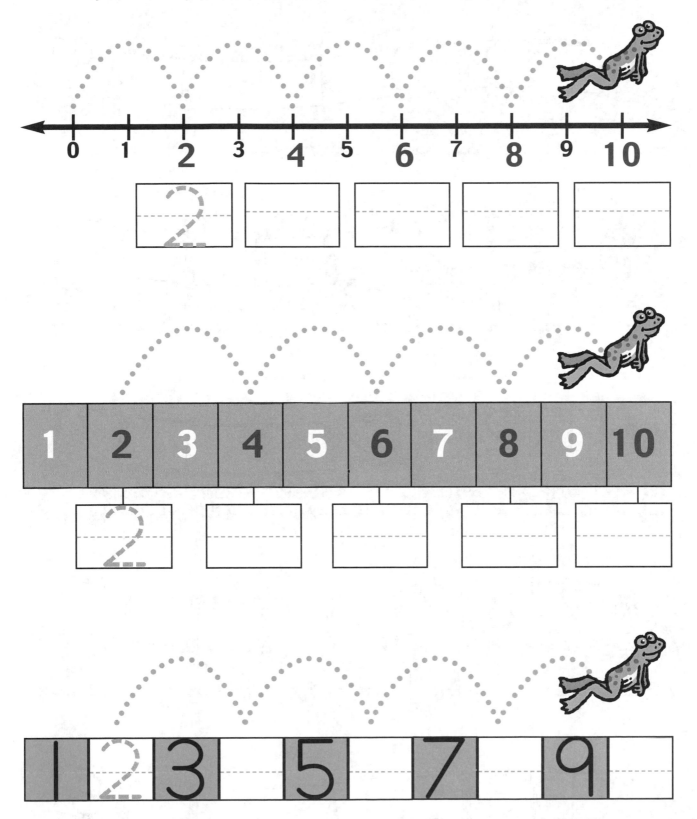

Find a Pattern

Write the missing number in each number pattern.

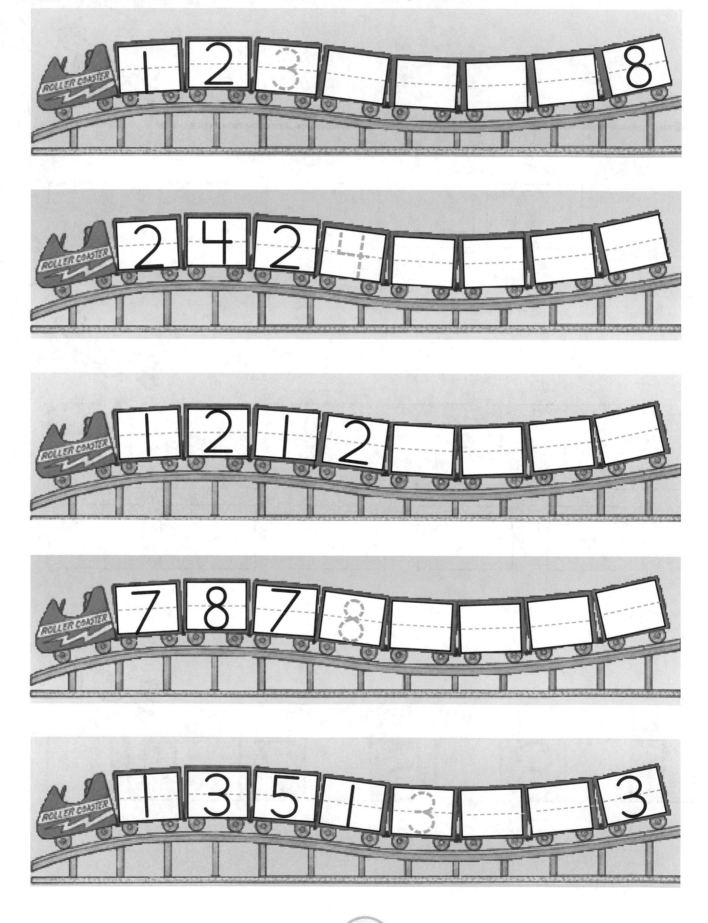

Find a Pattern

Draw and color the next shape in each pattern.

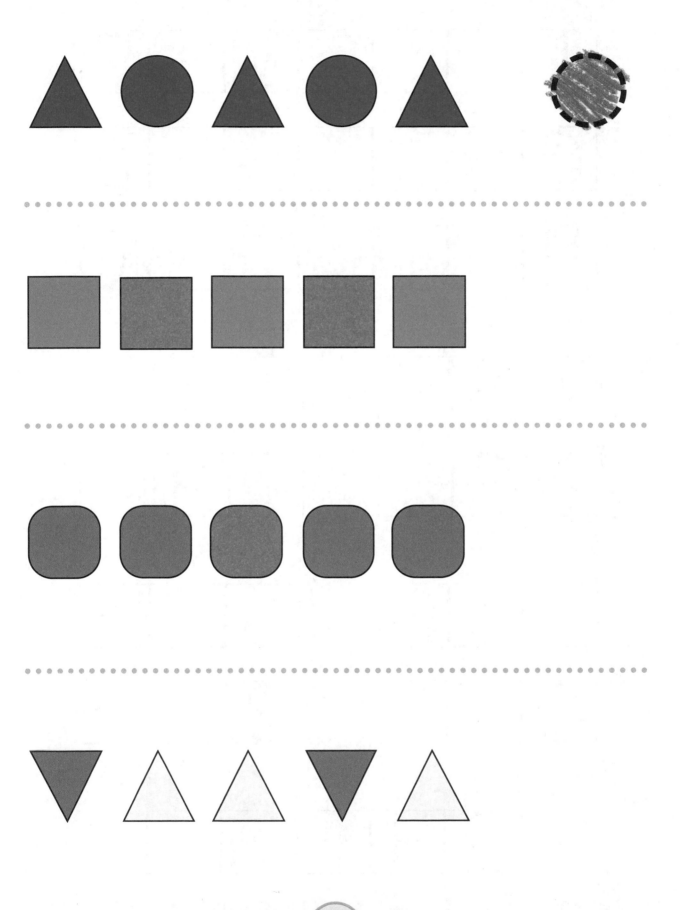

Write the missing numbers.

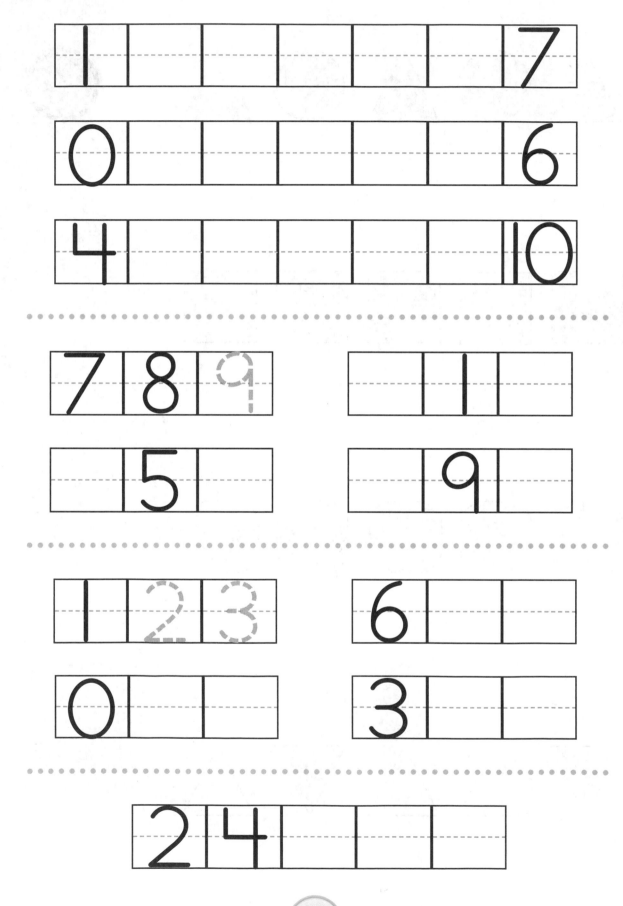

Count the objects. Write the numbers that tell how many of each.

- -

Draw and color the next shape in the pattern.

Sums to 6

Add the objects in each row. Write the numbers that tell how many in all.

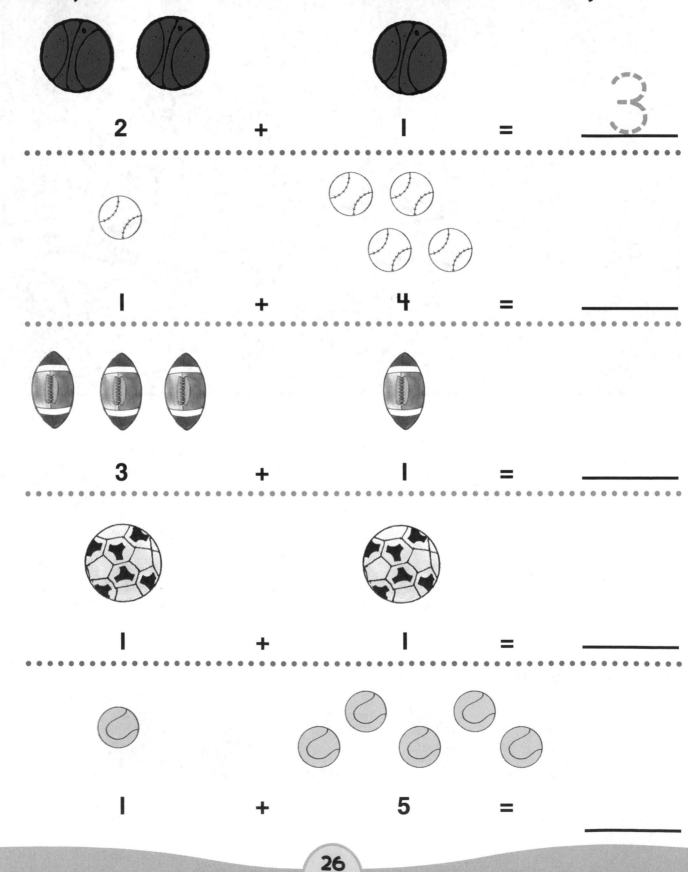

2   +   1   =   3

1   +   4   = ____

3   +   1   = ____

1   +   1   = ____

1   +   5   = ____

Add the objects in each row. Write the numbers that tell how many in all.

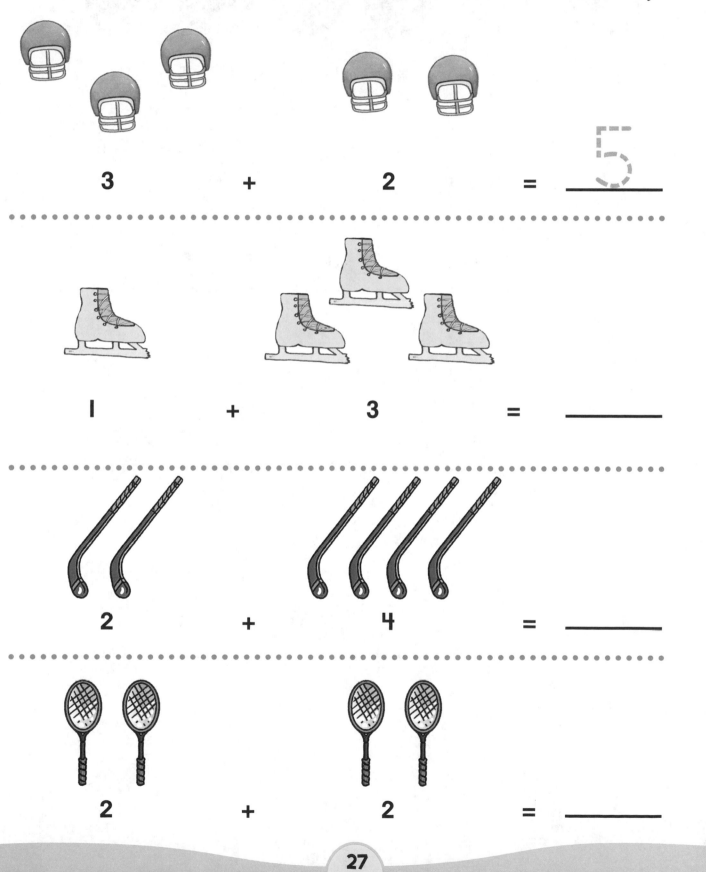

3   +   2   =   5

1   +   3   = ____

2   +   4   = ____

2   +   2   = ____

Sums of 5

Draw and color circles to show each number sentence.

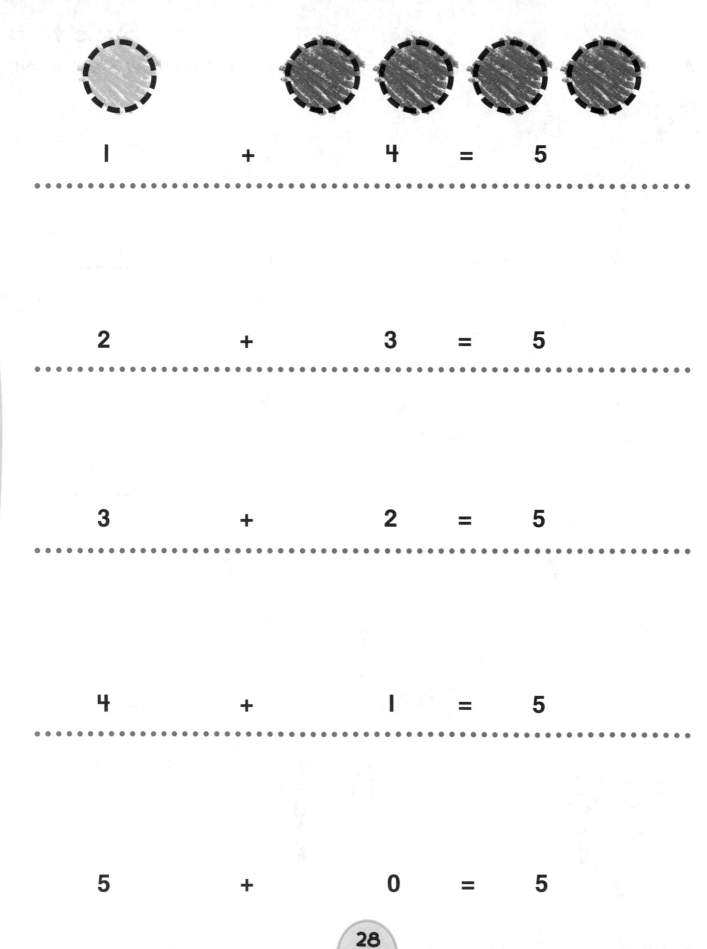

1 + 4 = 5

....

2 + 3 = 5

....

3 + 2 = 5

....

4 + 1 = 5

....

5 + 0 = 5

Draw and color circles to show each number sentence.

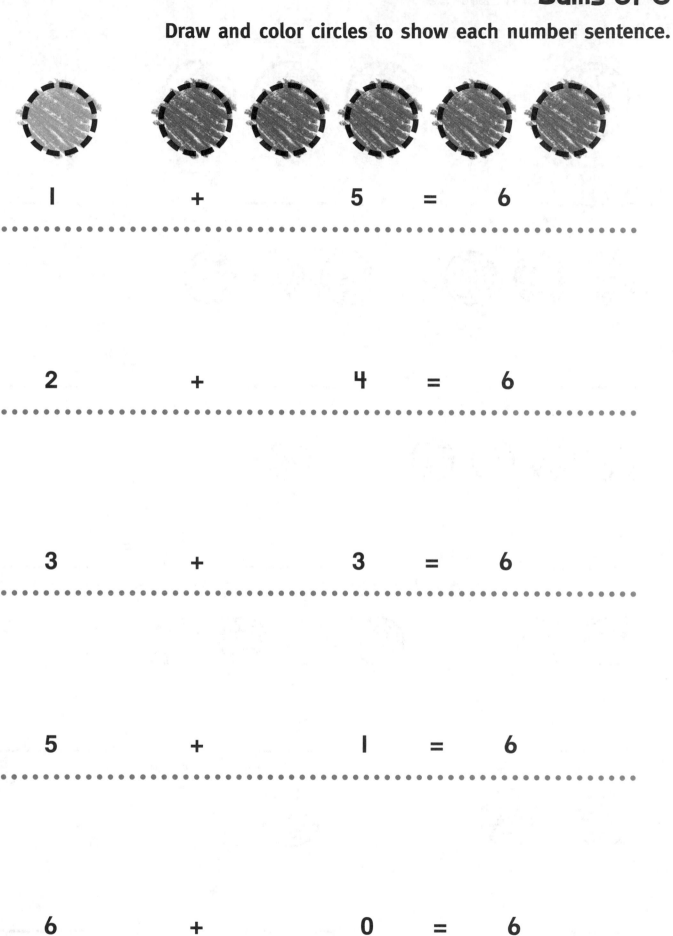

1 + 5 = 6

....

2 + 4 = 6

....

3 + 3 = 6

....

5 + 1 = 6

....

6 + 0 = 6

Number Sentences

Write the number sentences.

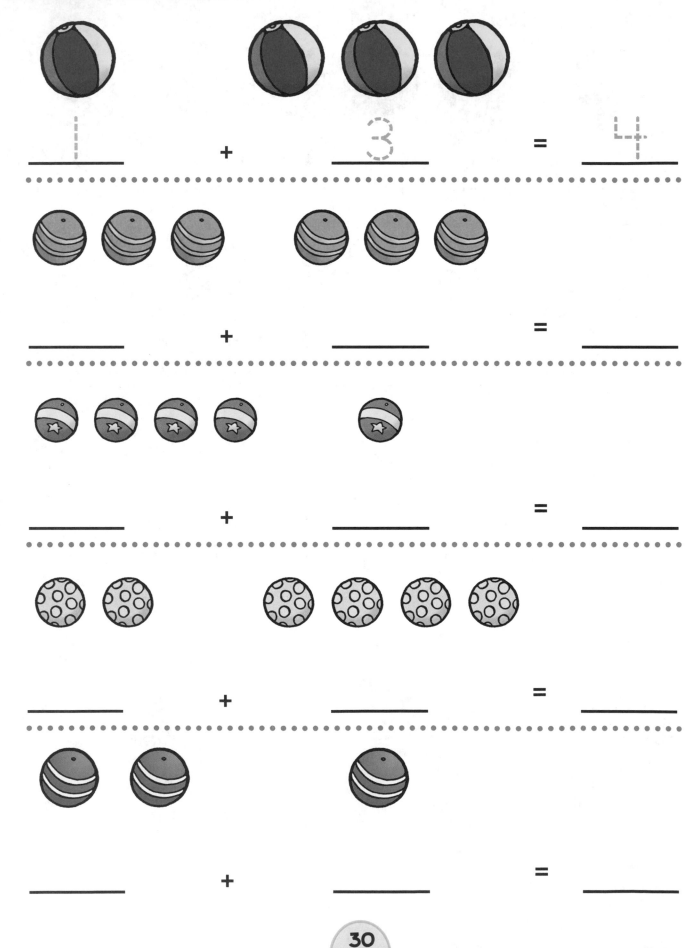

1 + 3 = 4

____ + ____ = ____

____ + ____ = ____

____ + ____ = ____

____ + ____ = ____

____ + ____ = ____

Write the number sentences.

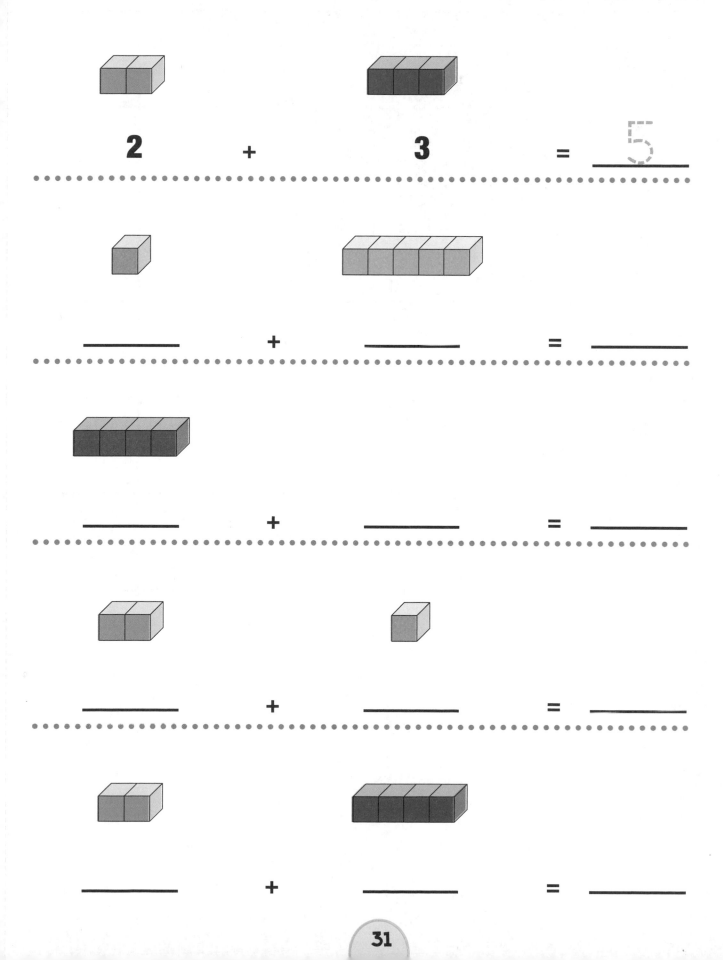

2 + **3** = 5

_____ + _____ = _____

_____ + _____ = _____

_____ + _____ = _____

_____ + _____ = _____

Using a Graph

Find the number of each object on the graph. Then write the sums.

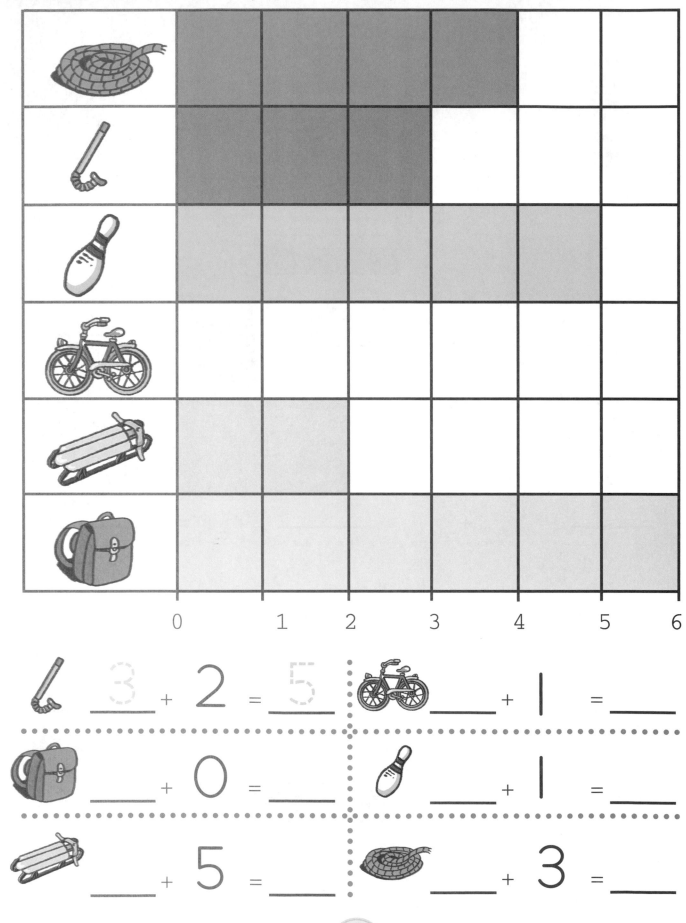

	0	1	2	3	4	5	6

3 + 2 = 5

____ + 1 = ____

____ + 0 = ____

____ + 1 = ____

____ + 5 = ____

____ + 3 = ____

32

Find the number of each object on the graph.
Then write the number that is added to equal each sum.

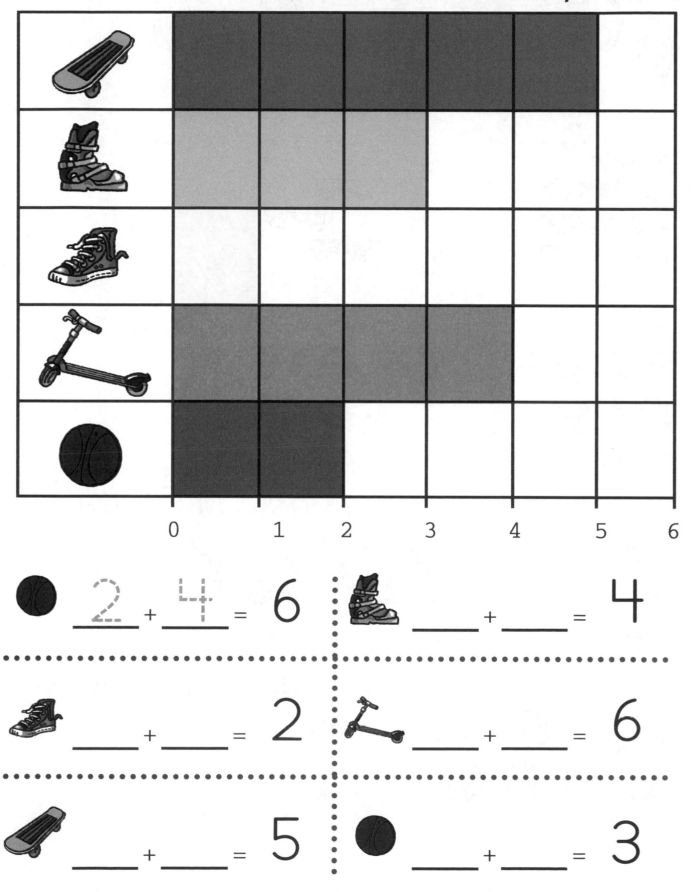

_2_ + _4_ = 6

___ + ___ = 4

___ + ___ = 2

___ + ___ = 6

___ + ___ = 5

___ + ___ = 3

Sums to 10

Add the objects in each row. Write the numbers that tell how many in all.

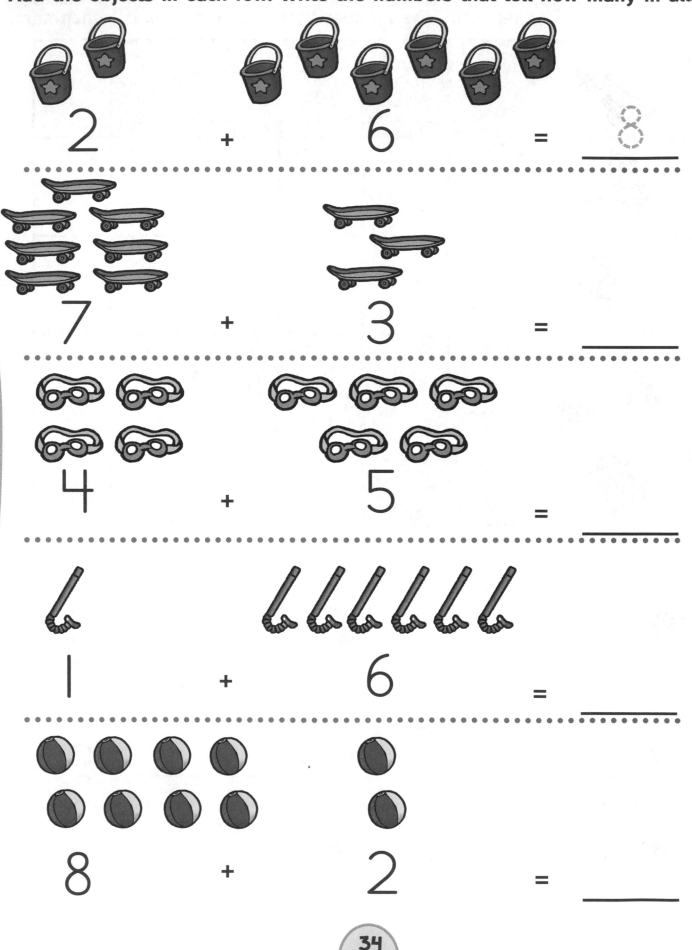

2 + 6 = 8

7 + 3 = ____

4 + 5 = ____

1 + 6 = ____

8 + 2 = ____

Write the number sentences that match the objects on the flags.

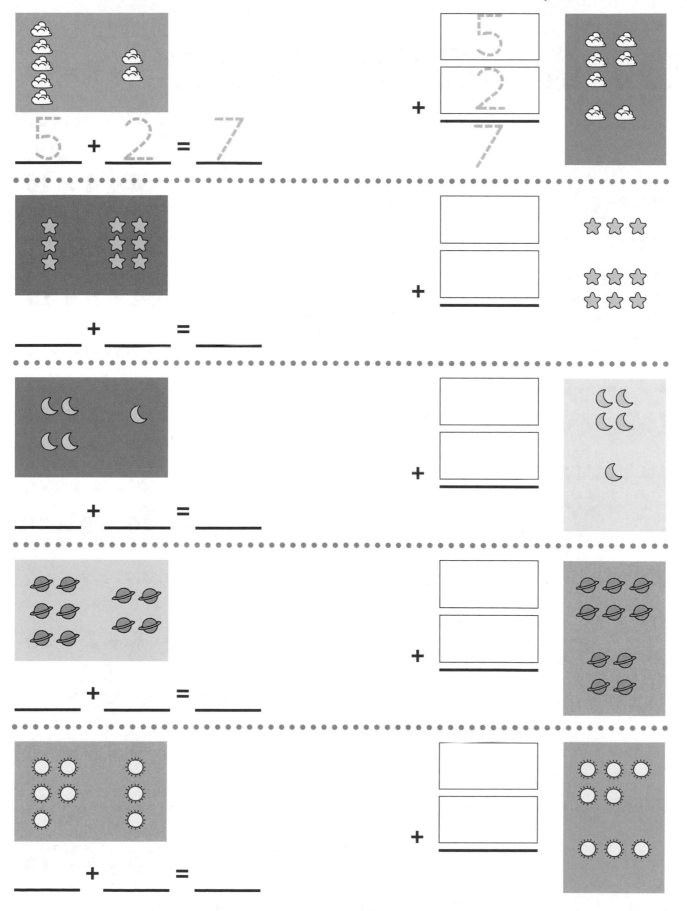

5 + 2 = 7

_____ + _____ = _____

_____ + _____ = _____

_____ + _____ = _____

_____ + _____ = _____

Sums of 10

Color the circles to show each number sentence.

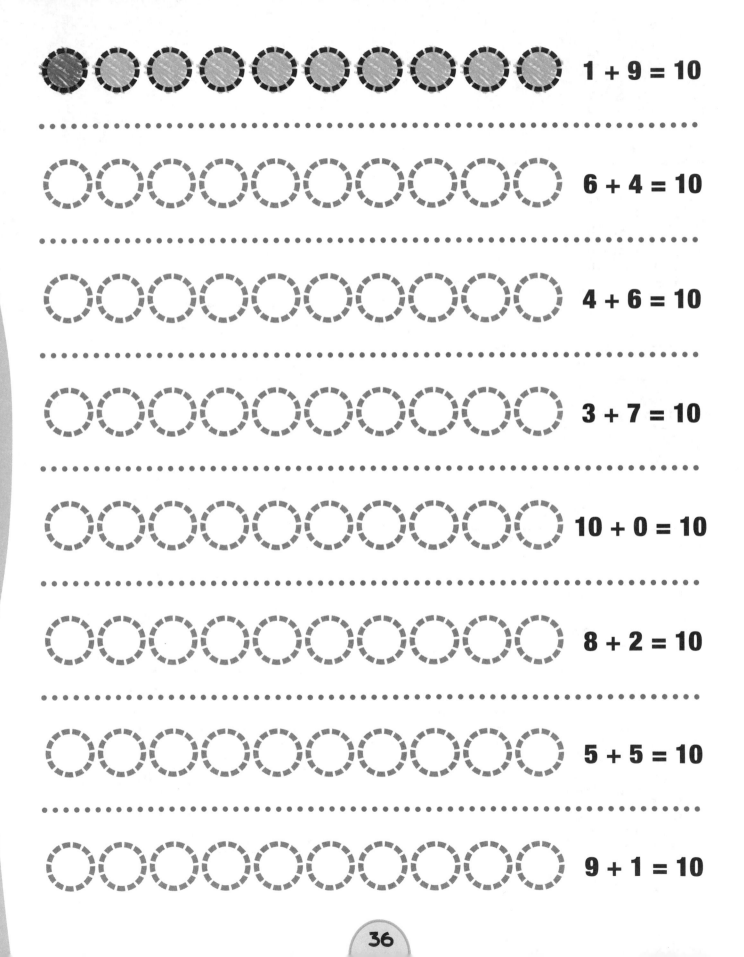

$1 + 9 = 10$

$6 + 4 = 10$

$4 + 6 = 10$

$3 + 7 = 10$

$10 + 0 = 10$

$8 + 2 = 10$

$5 + 5 = 10$

$9 + 1 = 10$

Sums of 10

Write the numbers that match the pictures. Then write the sums.

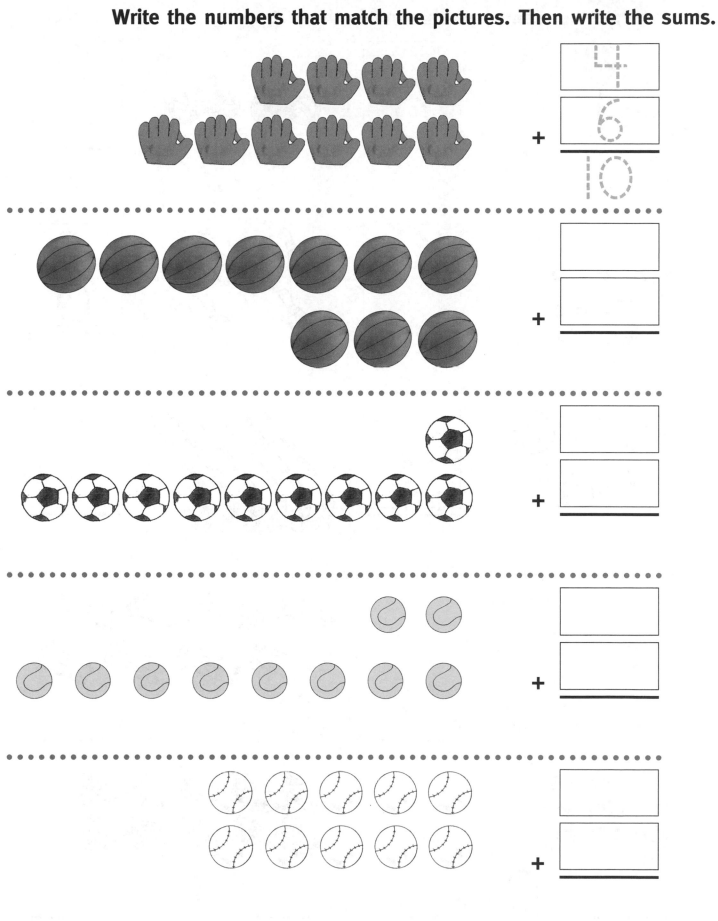

4 + 6 = 10

37

Adding Zero

Write the number sentences that match the pictures.

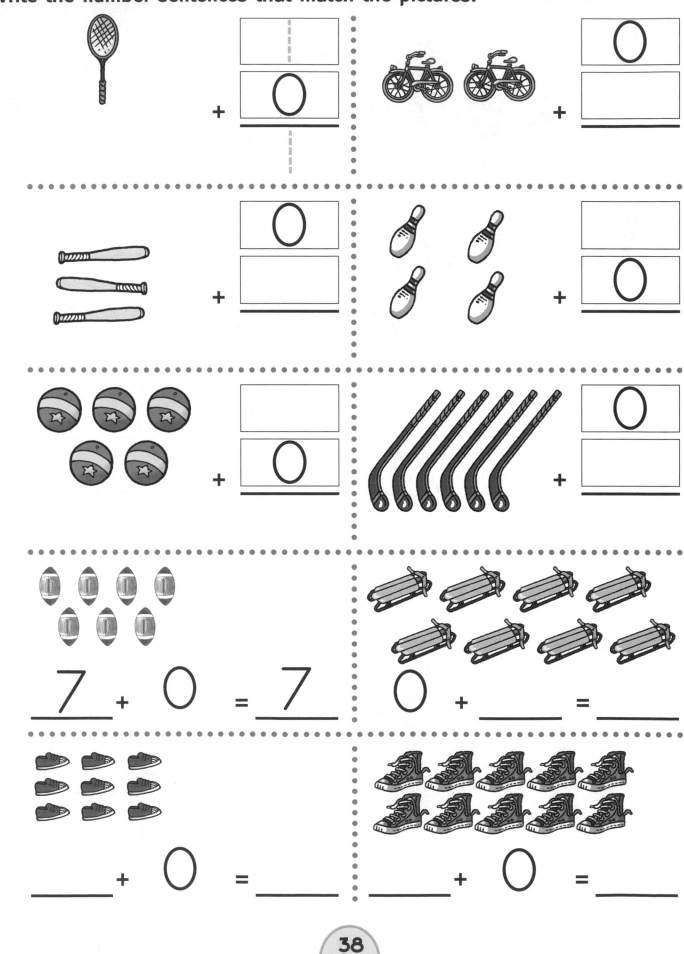

$7 + 0 = 7$

$0 + \rule{1cm}{0.4pt} = \rule{1cm}{0.4pt}$

$\rule{1cm}{0.4pt} + 0 = \rule{1cm}{0.4pt}$

$\rule{1cm}{0.4pt} + 0 = \rule{1cm}{0.4pt}$

38

Doubles

Write the number sentences that match the objects on the flags.

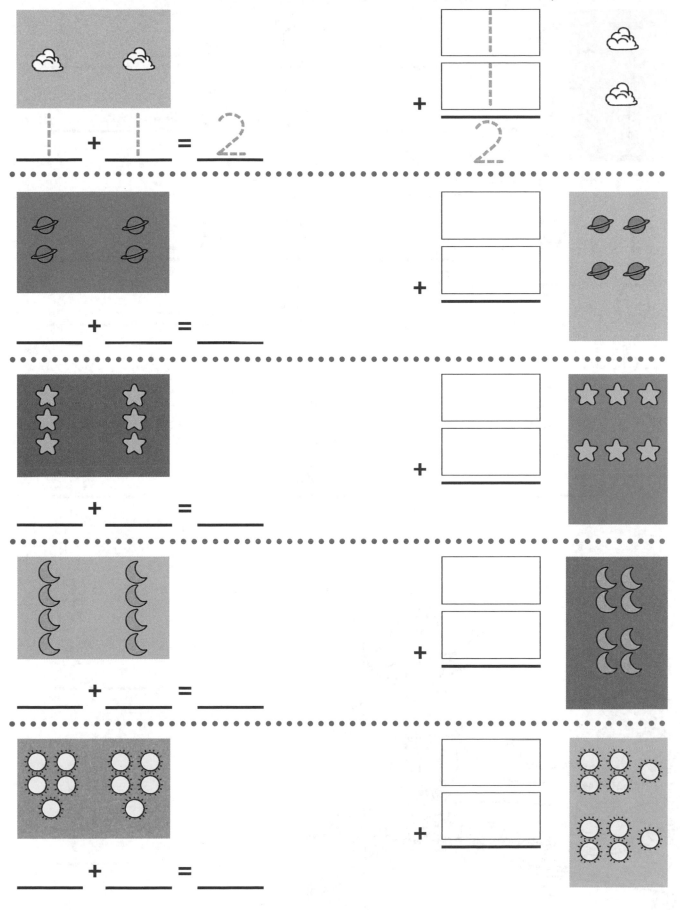

1 + 1 = 2

_____ + _____ = _____

_____ + _____ = _____

_____ + _____ = _____

_____ + _____ = _____

Unit 2 Review

Write the sums.

$7 + 3 = \underline{\hphantom{00}}$ $2 + 4 = \underline{\hphantom{00}}$

$1 + 1 = \underline{\hphantom{00}}$ $5 + 0 = \underline{\hphantom{00}}$

$3 + 6 = \underline{\hphantom{00}}$ $4 + 4 = \underline{\hphantom{00}}$

$1 + 9 = \underline{\hphantom{00}}$ $2 + 3 = \underline{\hphantom{00}}$

$0 + 7 = \underline{\hphantom{00}}$ $8 + 2 = \underline{\hphantom{00}}$

$$\begin{array}{r} 5 \\ + 4 \\ \hline \end{array}$$

$$\begin{array}{r} 3 \\ + 5 \\ \hline \end{array}$$

$$\begin{array}{r} 6 \\ + 1 \\ \hline \end{array}$$

$$\begin{array}{r} 4 \\ + 3 \\ \hline \end{array}$$

$$\begin{array}{r} 0 \\ + 4 \\ \hline \end{array}$$

Unit 2 Review

Find the number of each object on the graph. Complete the number sentences. Then draw a line from each number sentence to its model.

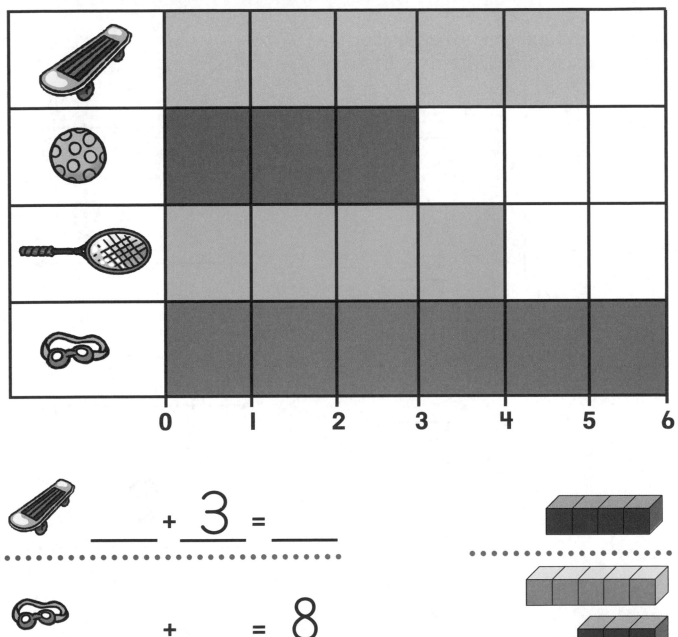

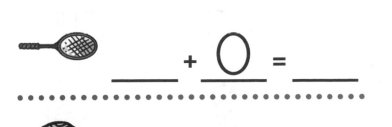 ____ + 3 = ____

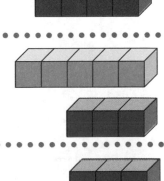

____ + ____ = 8

____ + 0 = ____

____ + ____ = 10

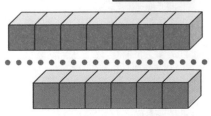

41

Subtract 1

First circle the number on the number line.
Then count back one. Write the difference.

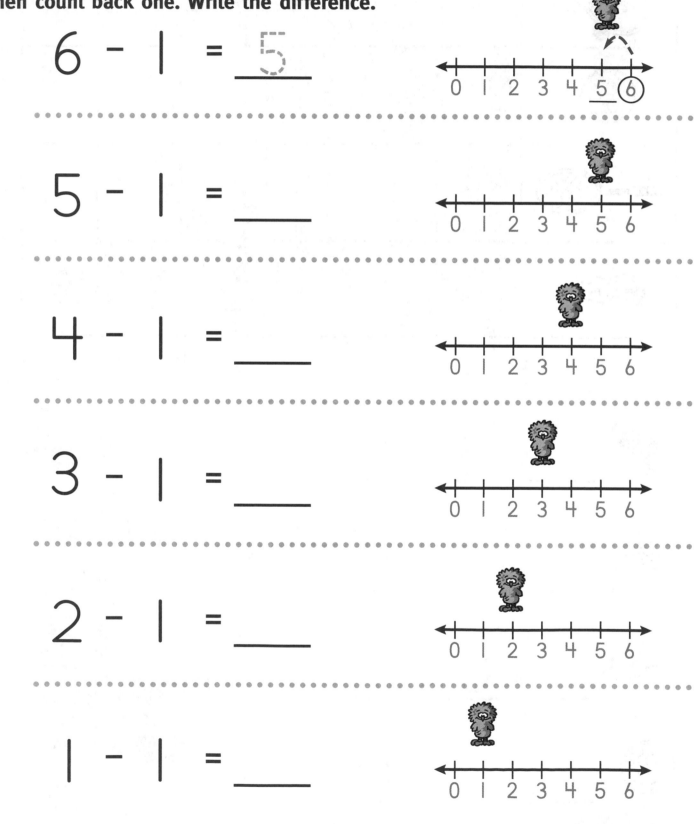

$6 - 1 = \underline{5}$

$5 - 1 = \underline{}$

$4 - 1 = \underline{}$

$3 - 1 = \underline{}$

$2 - 1 = \underline{}$

$1 - 1 = \underline{}$

First circle the number on the number line.
Then count back two. Write the difference.

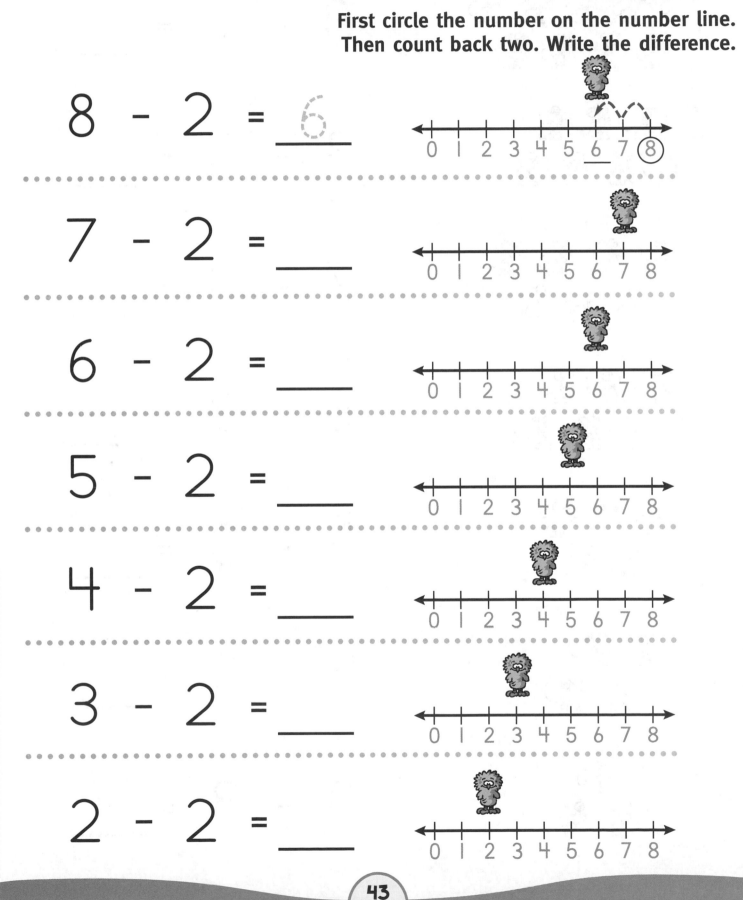

8 - 2 = _6_

7 - 2 = __

6 - 2 = __

5 - 2 = __

4 - 2 = __

3 - 2 = __

2 - 2 = __

Subtract 3

Cross out the animals to subtract. Write the differences.

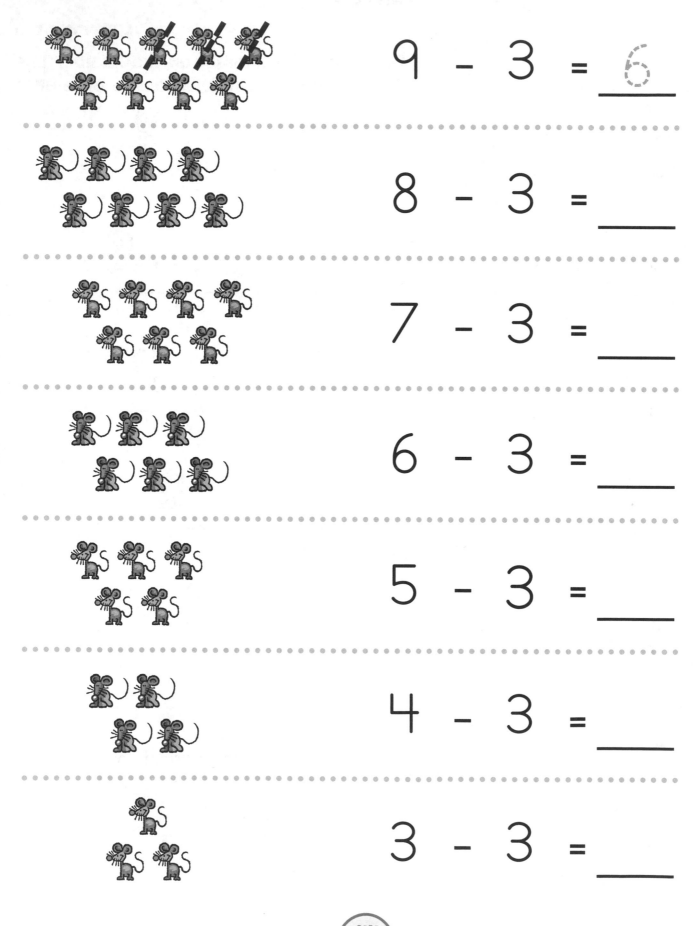

9 - 3 = _6_

8 - 3 = ___

7 - 3 = ___

6 - 3 = ___

5 - 3 = ___

4 - 3 = ___

3 - 3 = ___

Write how many of each animal. Then write the difference.

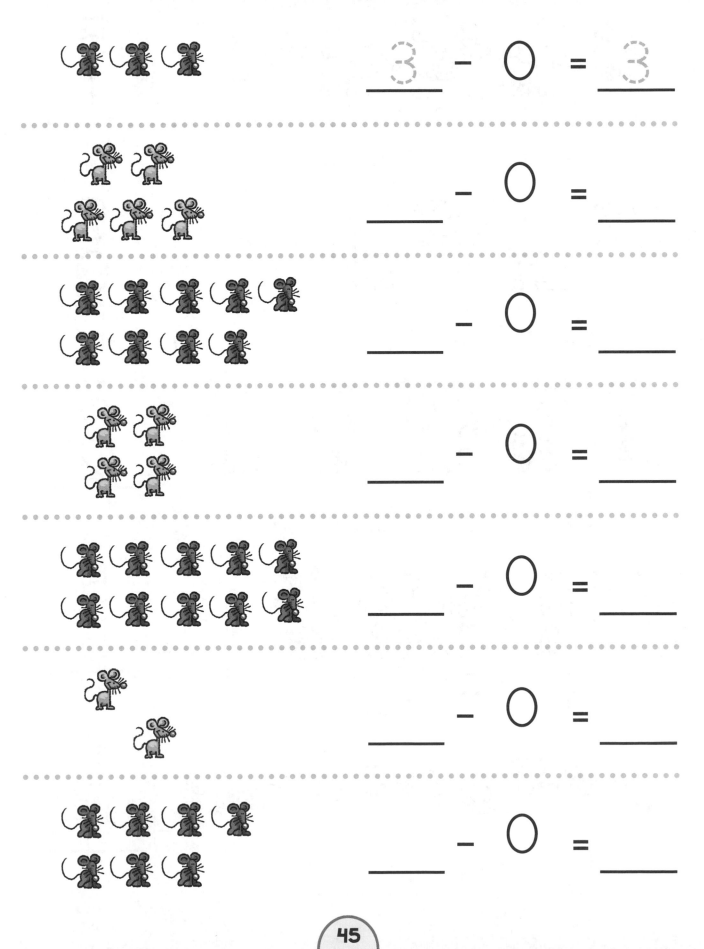

3 – 0 = 3

____ – 0 = ____

____ – 0 = ____

____ – 0 = ____

____ – 0 = ____

____ – 0 = ____

____ – 0 = ____

Differences from 5

Cross out the dogs to subtract. Write the differences.

5 - 1 = 4   5
                 - 1
                 ———
                   4

5 - 0 = ___   5
                 - 0
                 ———

5 - 2 = ___   5
                 - 2
                 ———

5 - 5 = ___   5
                 - 5
                 ———

5 - 4 = ___   5
                 - 4
                 ———

Cross out the cats to subtract. Write the differences.

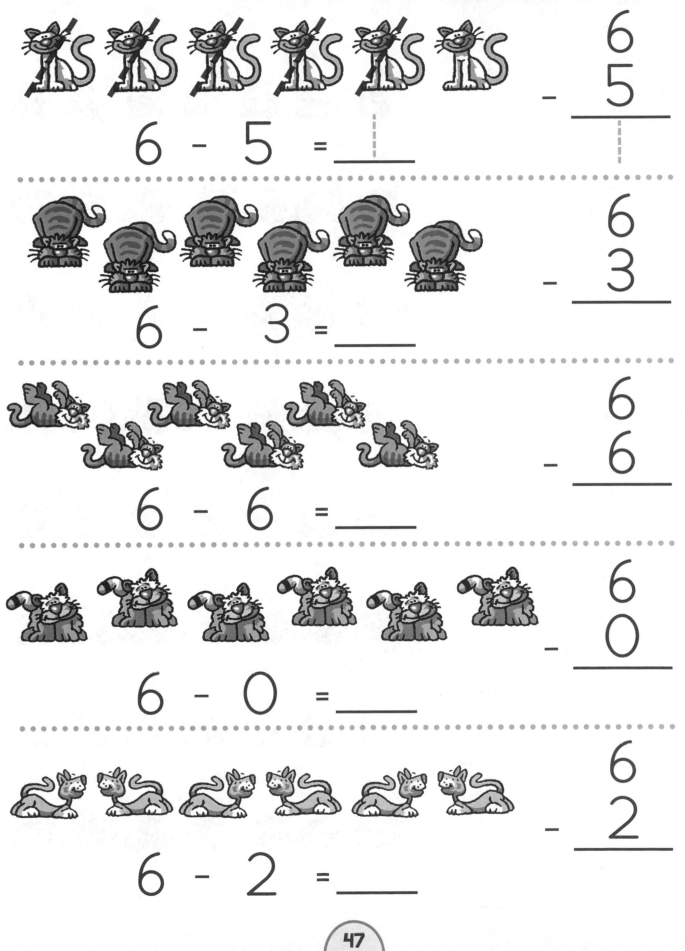

6 - 5 = ___   6
              - 5
              ___

6 - 3 = ___   6
              - 3
              ___

6 - 6 = ___   6
              - 6
              ___

6 - 0 = ___   6
              - 0
              ___

6 - 2 = ___   6
              - 2
              ___

Differences from 7

Write the differences. Draw a line from each subtraction problem to its model.

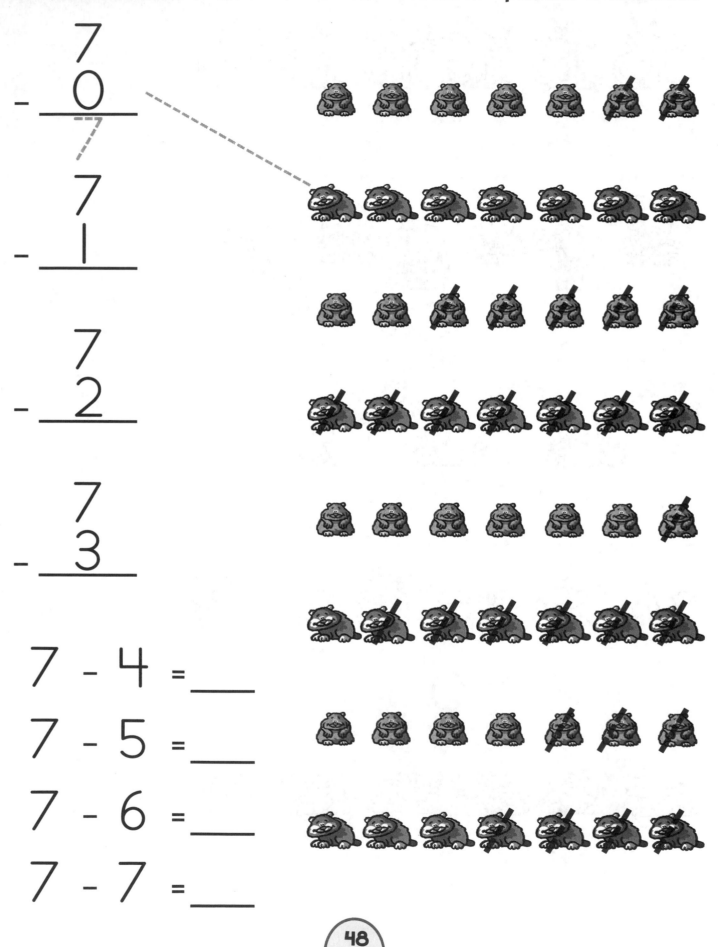

$$7 - 4 = \_\_$$

$$7 - 5 = \_\_$$

$$7 - 6 = \_\_$$

$$7 - 7 = \_\_$$

Write the differences. Draw a line from each subtraction problem to its model.

$$
\begin{array}{r} 8 \\ -\ 0 \\ \hline 8 \end{array}
$$

$$
\begin{array}{r} 8 \\ -\ 1 \\ \hline \end{array}
$$

$$
\begin{array}{r} 8 \\ -\ 2 \\ \hline \end{array}
$$

$$
\begin{array}{r} 8 \\ -\ 3 \\ \hline \end{array}
$$

8 – 4 = ___

8 – 5 = ___

8 – 6 = ___

8 – 7 = ___

8 – 8 = ___

Differences from 9

Cross out the eggs to subtract. Write the differences.

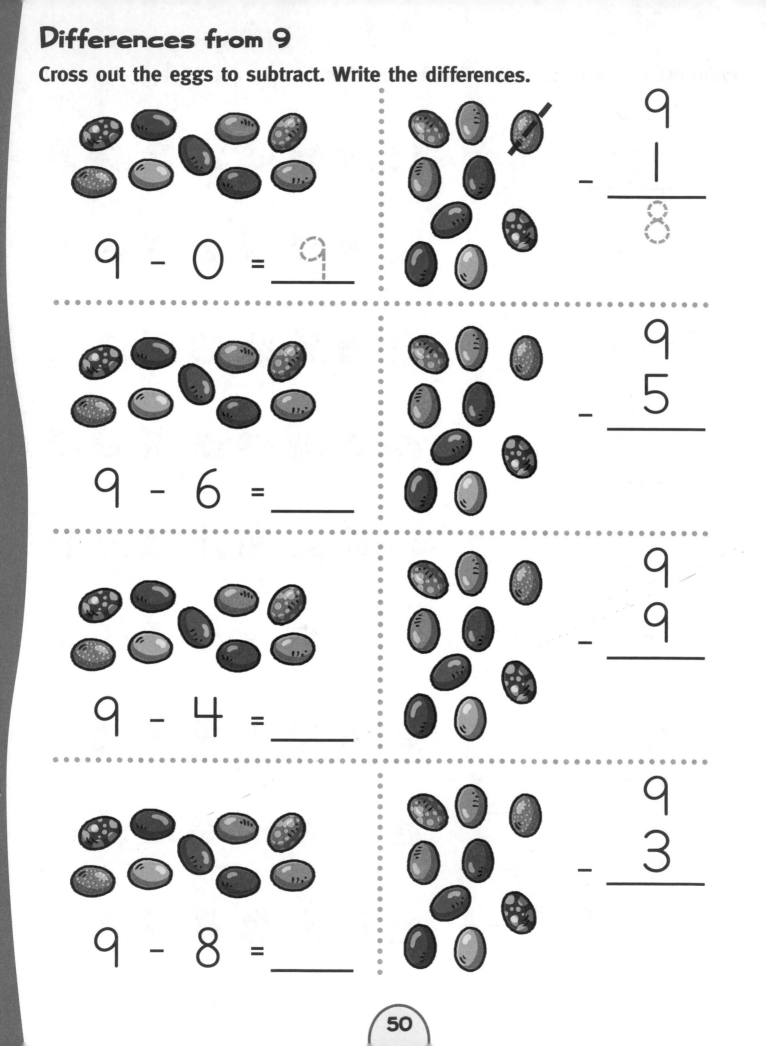

9 - 0 = __9__

$$\begin{array}{r} 9 \\ -\ 1 \\ \hline 8 \end{array}$$

9 - 6 = ____

$$\begin{array}{r} 9 \\ -\ 5 \\ \hline \end{array}$$

9 - 4 = ____

$$\begin{array}{r} 9 \\ -\ 9 \\ \hline \end{array}$$

9 - 8 = ____

$$\begin{array}{r} 9 \\ -\ 3 \\ \hline \end{array}$$

Differences from 10

Draw a line to the matching model on the left.
Write the differences on the right.

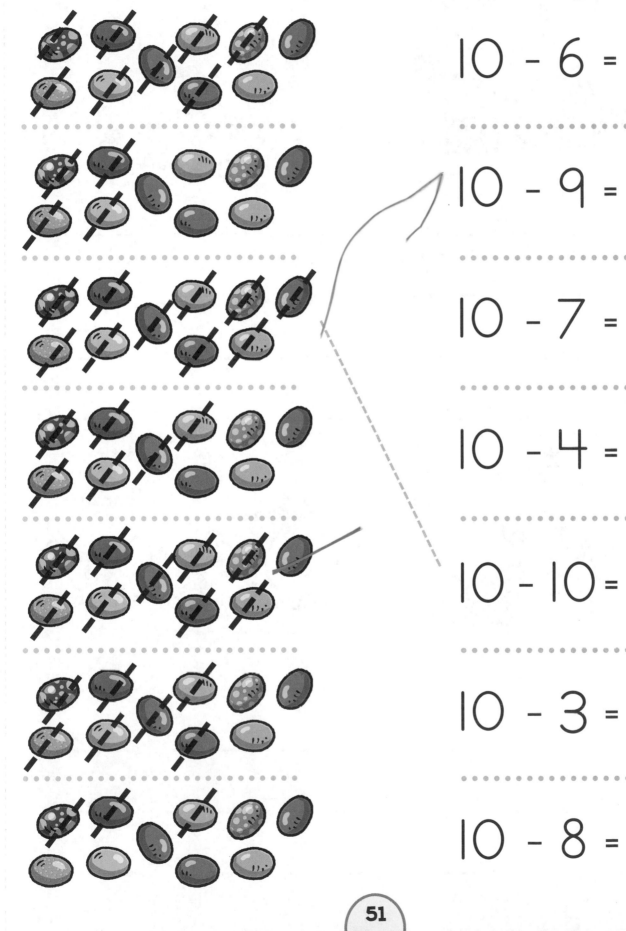

$10 - 6 = \underline{}$

$10 - 9 = \underline{}$

$10 - 7 = \underline{}$

$10 - 4 = \underline{}$

$10 - 10 = \underline{}$

$10 - 3 = \underline{}$

$10 - 8 = \underline{}$

Fact Families to 5

Write the fact family for each set of numbers.

3

1 + 2 = 3

2 + 1 = 3

3 − 2 = 1

3 − 1 = 2

4

___ + ___ = ___

___ + ___ = ___

___ − ___ = ___

___ − ___ = ___

5

___ + ___ = ___

___ + ___ = ___

___ − ___ = ___

___ − ___ = ___

5

___ + ___ = ___

___ + ___ = ___

___ − ___ = ___

___ − ___ = ___

Write the fact family for each set of numbers.

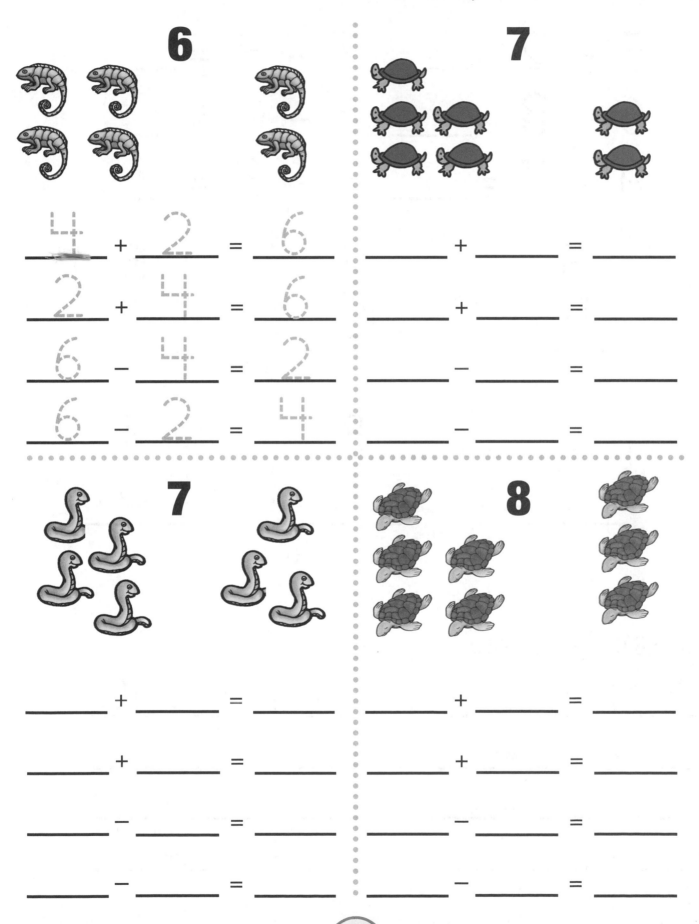

6

$$4 + 2 = 6$$
$$2 + 4 = 6$$
$$6 - 4 = 2$$
$$6 - 2 = 4$$

7

___ + ___ = ___
___ + ___ = ___
___ − ___ = ___
___ − ___ = ___

7

___ + ___ = ___
___ + ___ = ___
___ − ___ = ___
___ − ___ = ___

8

___ + ___ = ___
___ + ___ = ___
___ − ___ = ___
___ − ___ = ___

Write the differences.

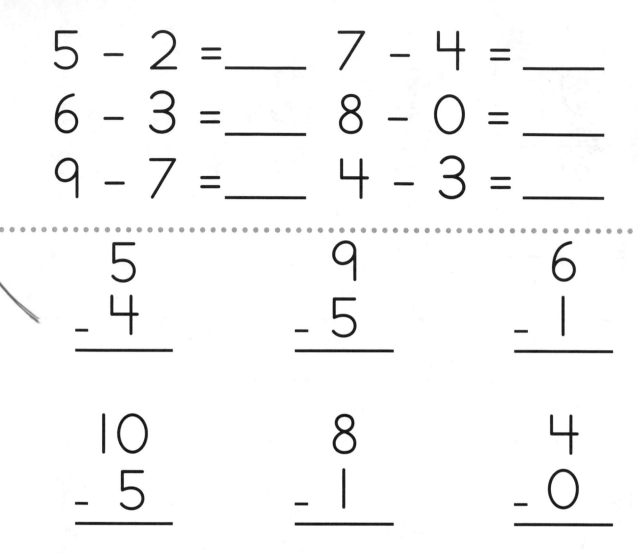

$5 - 2 =$ ___ $7 - 4 =$ ___

$6 - 3 =$ ___ $8 - 0 =$ ___

$9 - 7 =$ ___ $4 - 3 =$ ___

$$
\begin{array}{r} 5 \\ -\ 4 \\ \hline \end{array}
\qquad
\begin{array}{r} 9 \\ -\ 5 \\ \hline \end{array}
\qquad
\begin{array}{r} 6 \\ -\ 1 \\ \hline \end{array}
$$

$$
\begin{array}{r} 10 \\ -\ 5 \\ \hline \end{array}
\qquad
\begin{array}{r} 8 \\ -\ 1 \\ \hline \end{array}
\qquad
\begin{array}{r} 4 \\ -\ 0 \\ \hline \end{array}
$$

Complete the fact families.

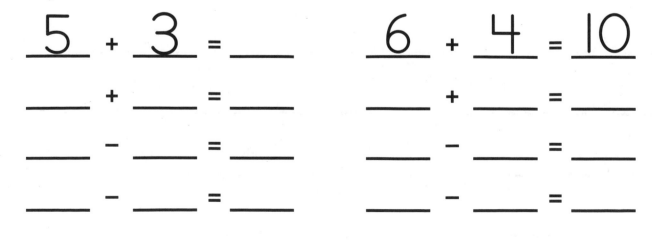

5 + 3 = ___   6 + 4 = 10

___ + ___ = ___   ___ + ___ = ___

___ − ___ = ___   ___ − ___ = ___

___ − ___ = ___   ___ − ___ = ___

Unit 3 Review

Choose the operation. Then write the number sentence for each picture.

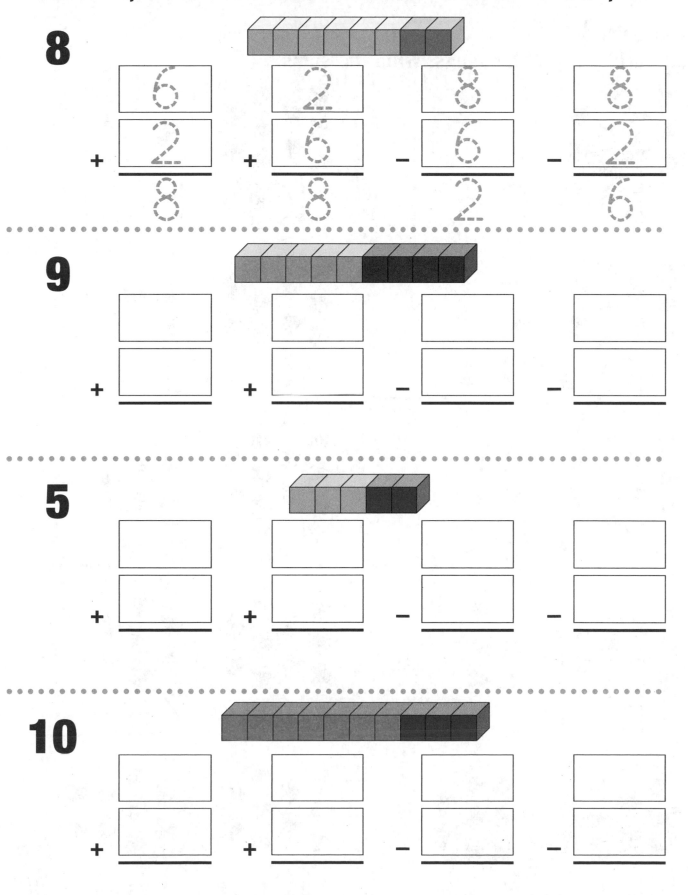

8

$$+\ \frac{\begin{array}{r}6\\2\end{array}}{8}$$

$$+\ \frac{\begin{array}{r}2\\6\end{array}}{8}$$

$$-\ \frac{\begin{array}{r}8\\6\end{array}}{2}$$

$$-\ \frac{\begin{array}{r}8\\2\end{array}}{6}$$

9

5

10

Numbers to 19

Count each group of ladybugs. Write the sums.

$10 + 0 = \underline{10}$

$10 + 1 = \underline{11}$

$10 + 2 = \underline{}$

$10 + 3 = \underline{}$

$10 + 4 = \underline{}$

$10 + 5 = \underline{}$

$10 + 6 = \underline{}$

$10 + 7 = \underline{}$

$10 + 8 = \underline{}$

$10 + 9 = \underline{}$

Count each group of bees.
Write the numbers that tell how many tens and ones.

10 + 4 = 14

10 + 0 = 10

_____ + _____ = 19

_____ + _____ = 13

_____ + _____ = 15

_____ + _____ = 17

_____ + _____ = 11

_____ + _____ = 18

Tens

Count how many tens. Then write the numbers.

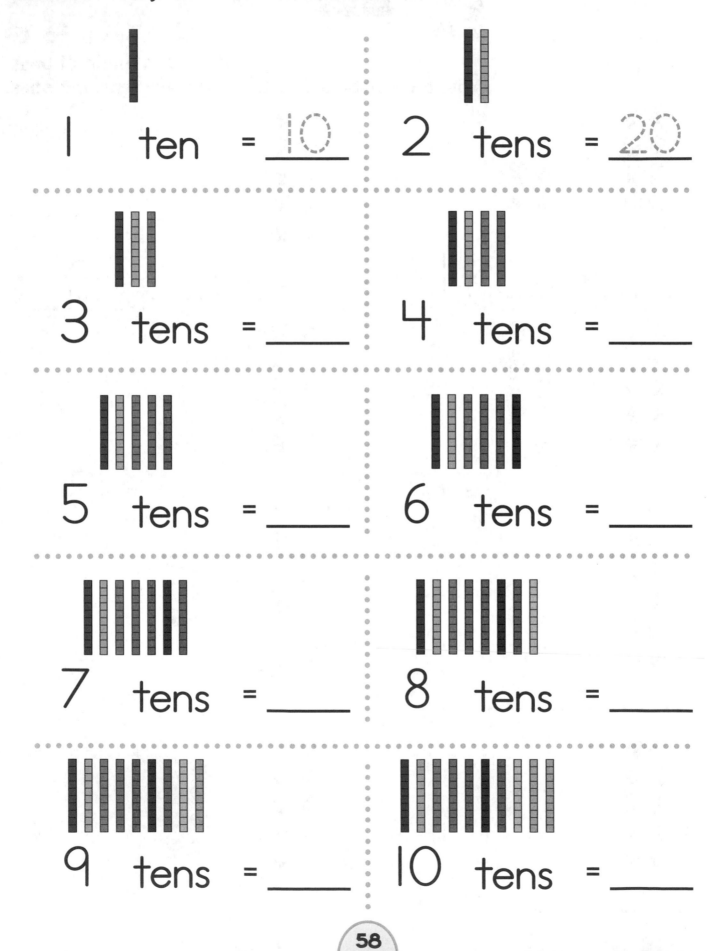

1 ten = 10

2 tens = 20

3 tens = ___

4 tens = ___

5 tens = ___

6 tens = ___

7 tens = ___

8 tens = ___

9 tens = ___

10 tens = ___

Add the tens. Then write the sums.

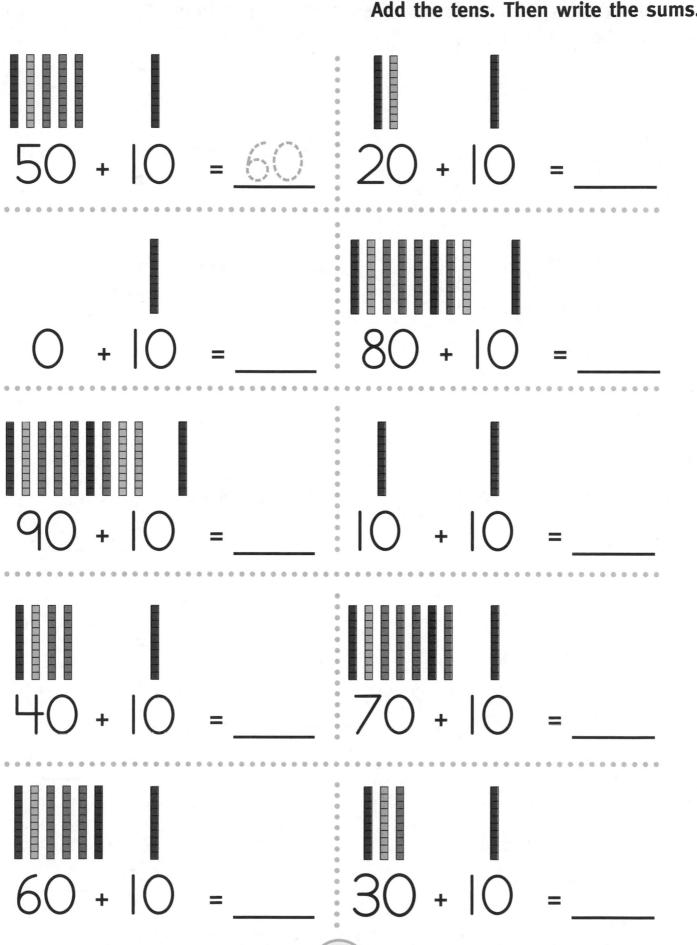

50 + 10 = 60

20 + 10 = ___

0 + 10 = ___

80 + 10 = ___

90 + 10 = ___

10 + 10 = ___

40 + 10 = ___

70 + 10 = ___

60 + 10 = ___

30 + 10 = ___

Tens and Ones to 20

Write how many tens and ones. Then write the numbers.

Tens	Ones
1	6

= 16

Tens	Ones

= ___

Tens	Ones

= ___

Tens	Ones

= ___

Tens	Ones

= ___

Tens	Ones

= ___

Tens	Ones

= ___

Tens	Ones

= ___

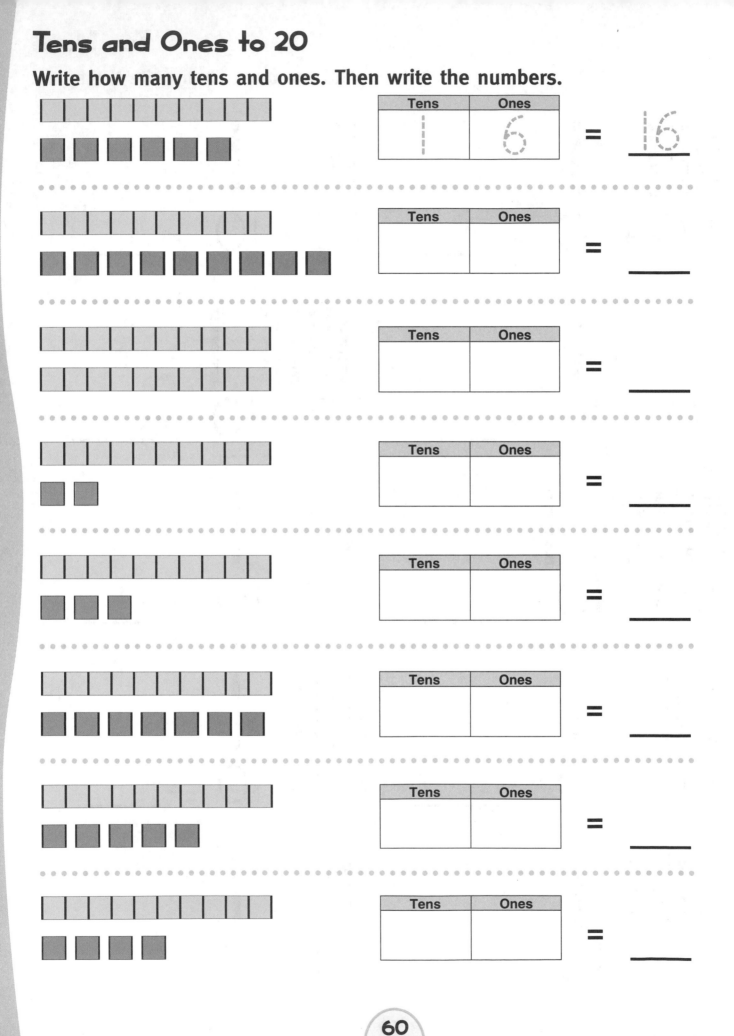

Write how many tens and ones. Then write the numbers.

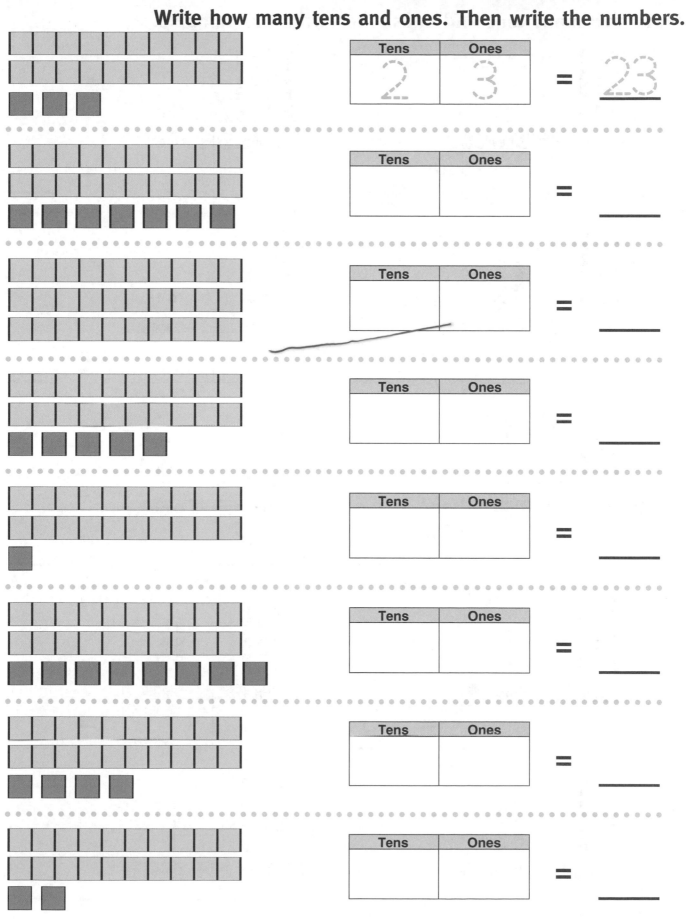

Tens	Ones
2	3

= 23

Tens	Ones

= ____

Tens	Ones

= ____

Tens	Ones

= ____

Tens	Ones

= ____

Tens	Ones

= ____

Tens	Ones

= ____

Tens	Ones

= ____

Tens and Ones to 40

Write how many tens and ones. Then write the numbers.

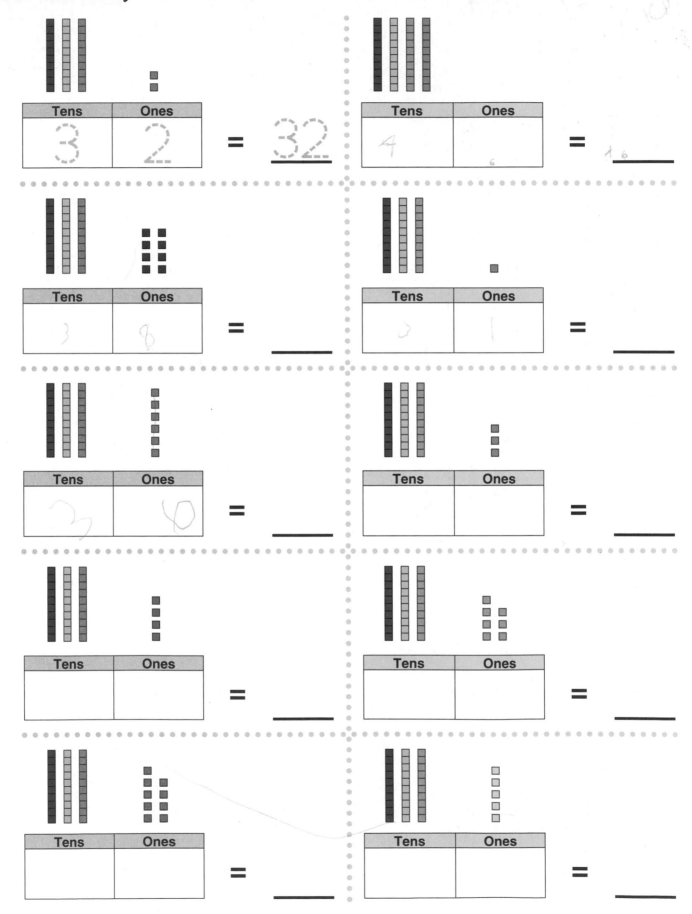

Tens	Ones
3	2

= 32

Tens	Ones
4	6

= 46

Tens	Ones
3	8

= ___

Tens	Ones
3	1

= ___

Tens	Ones
3	0

= ___

Tens	Ones

= ___

Tens	Ones

= ___

Tens	Ones

= ___

Tens	Ones

= ___

Tens	Ones

= ___

Write how many tens and ones. Then write the numbers.

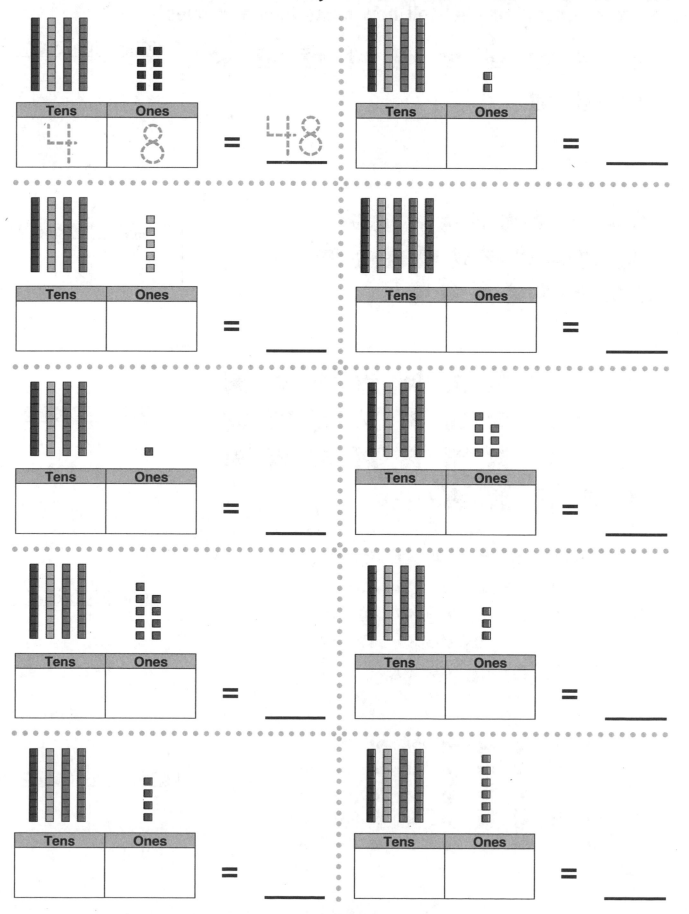

Tens	Ones
4	8

= _48_

Tens	Ones

= ____

Tens	Ones

= ____

Tens	Ones

= ____

Tens	Ones

= ____

Tens	Ones

= ____

Tens	Ones

= ____

Tens	Ones

= ____

Tens	Ones

= ____

Tens	Ones

= ____

Groups of Ten

Circle groups of ten.
Then write the numbers that tell how many tens and ones.

Tens	Ones
1	3

Tens	Ones

Tens	Ones

Tens	Ones

Tens	Ones

Circle groups of ten.
Then write the numbers that tell how many tens and ones.

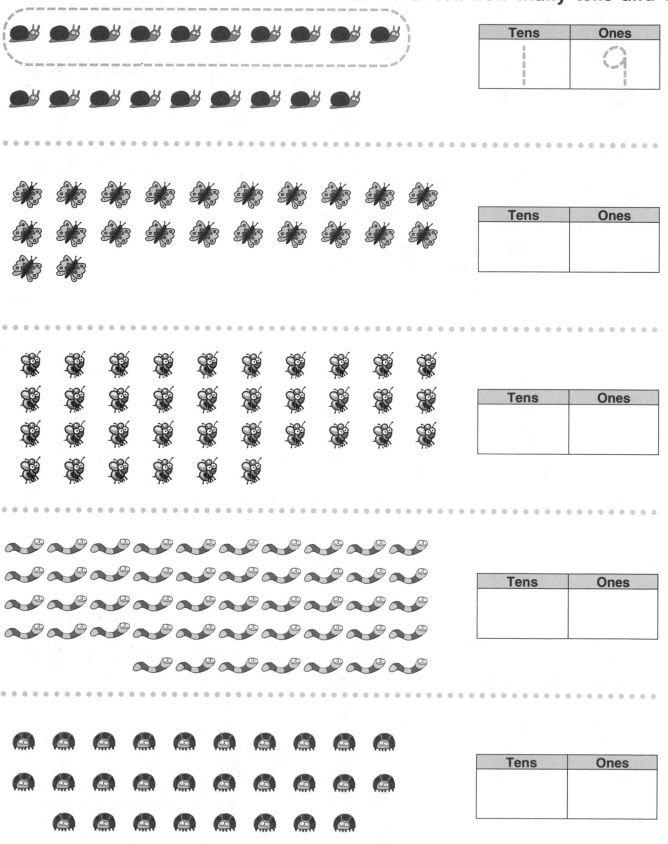

Tens	Ones
1	9

Tens	Ones

Tens	Ones

Tens	Ones

Tens	Ones

Guess and Check

Guess the nearest ten. Then count and write how many in each group.

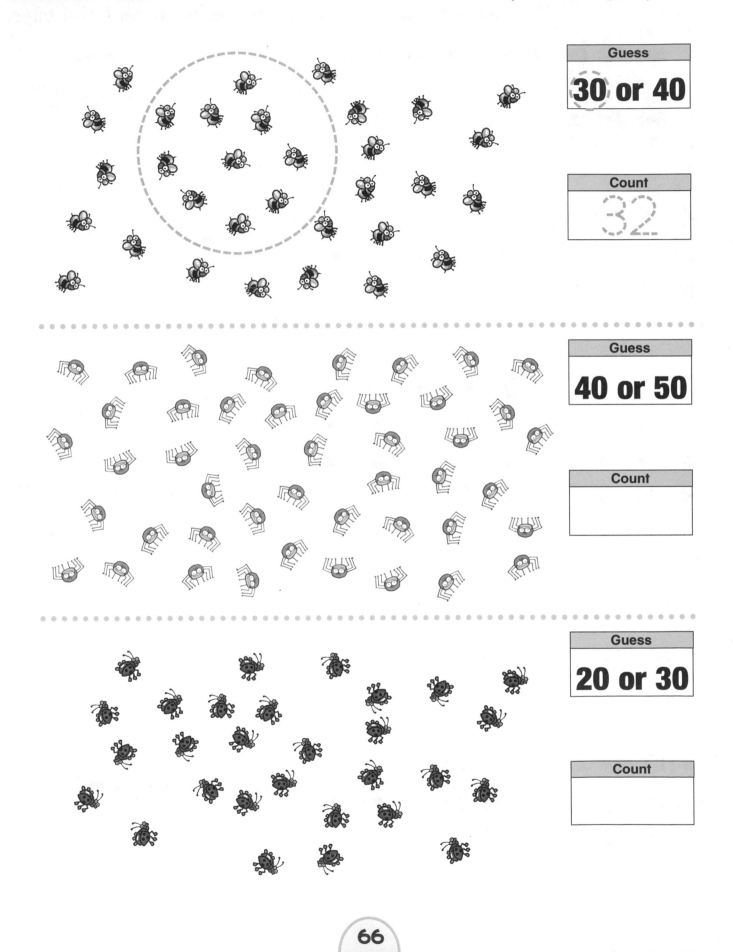

Guess
30 or 40

Count
32

Guess
40 or 50

Count

Guess
20 or 30

Count

Guess the nearest ten. Then count and write how many in each group.

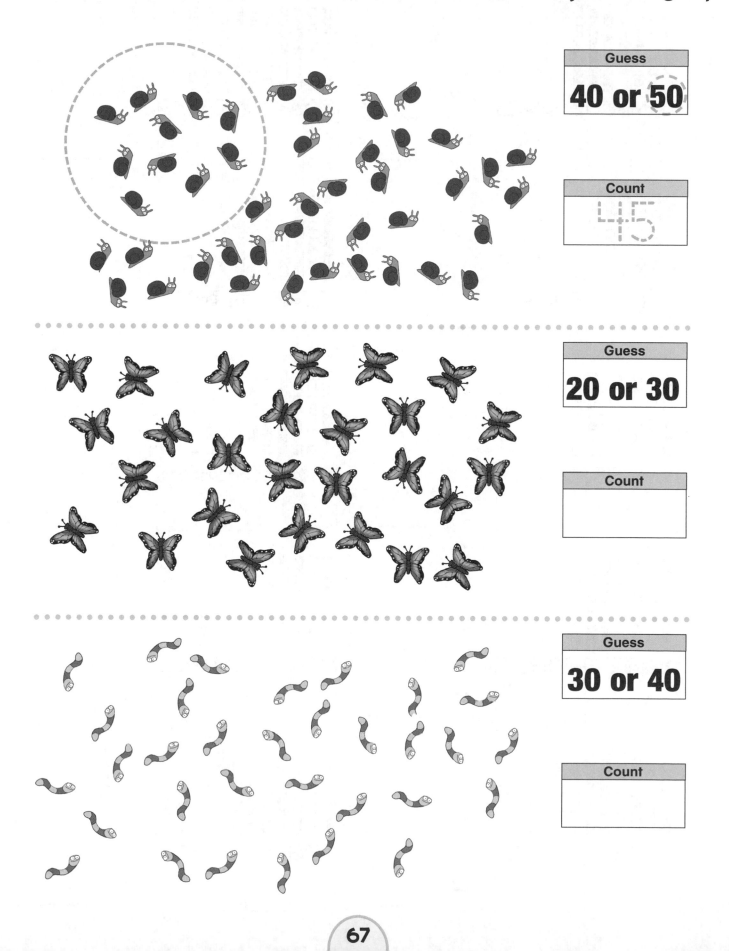

Guess
40 or (50)

Count
45

Guess
20 or 30

Count

Guess
30 or 40

Count

Tens and Ones to 100

Write how many tens and ones. Then write the numbers.

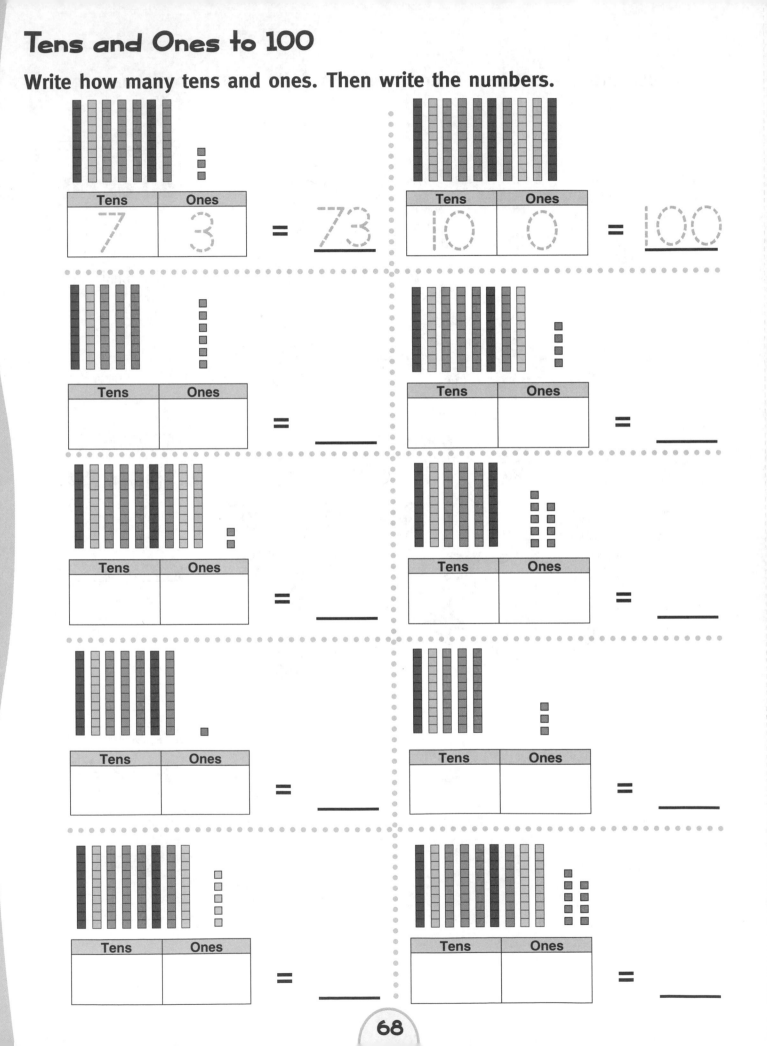

Tens	Ones
7	3

= 73

Tens	Ones
10	0

= 100

Tens	Ones

= ___

Tens	Ones

= ___

Tens	Ones

= ___

Tens	Ones

= ___

Tens	Ones

= ___

Tens	Ones

= ___

Tens	Ones

= ___

Tens	Ones

= ___

Write how many tens and ones. Then write the numbers.

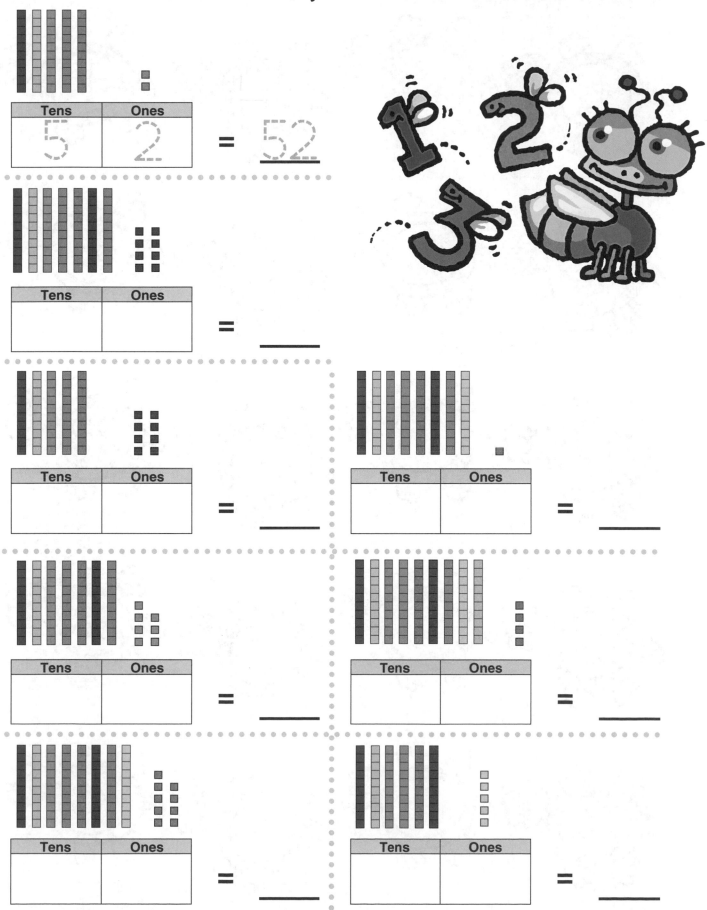

Tens	Ones
5	2

= 52

Tens	Ones

= ___

Tens	Ones

= ___

Tens	Ones

= ___

Tens	Ones

= ___

Tens	Ones

= ___

Tens	Ones

= ___

Tens	Ones

= ___

Missing Numbers

Write the missing numbers.

Write the numbers that come just before and just after the ones shown.

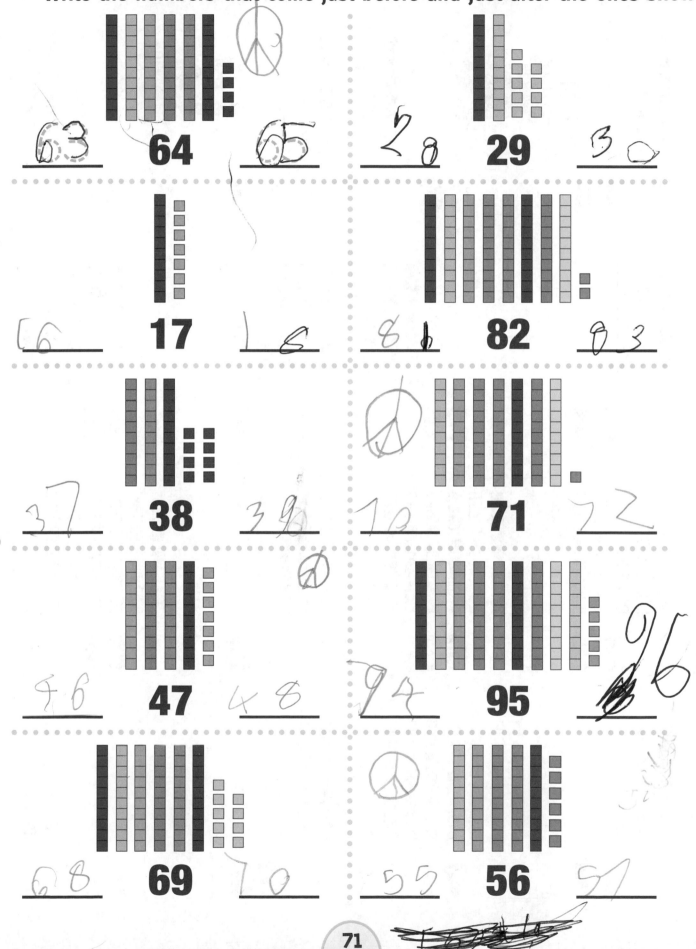

63   **64**   65   28   **29**   30

16   **17**   18   81   **82**   83

37   **38**   39   70   **71**   72

46   **47**   48   94   **95**   96

68   **69**   70   55   **56**   57

71

Comparing Numbers

Compare the numbers. Then write > or < in each box.

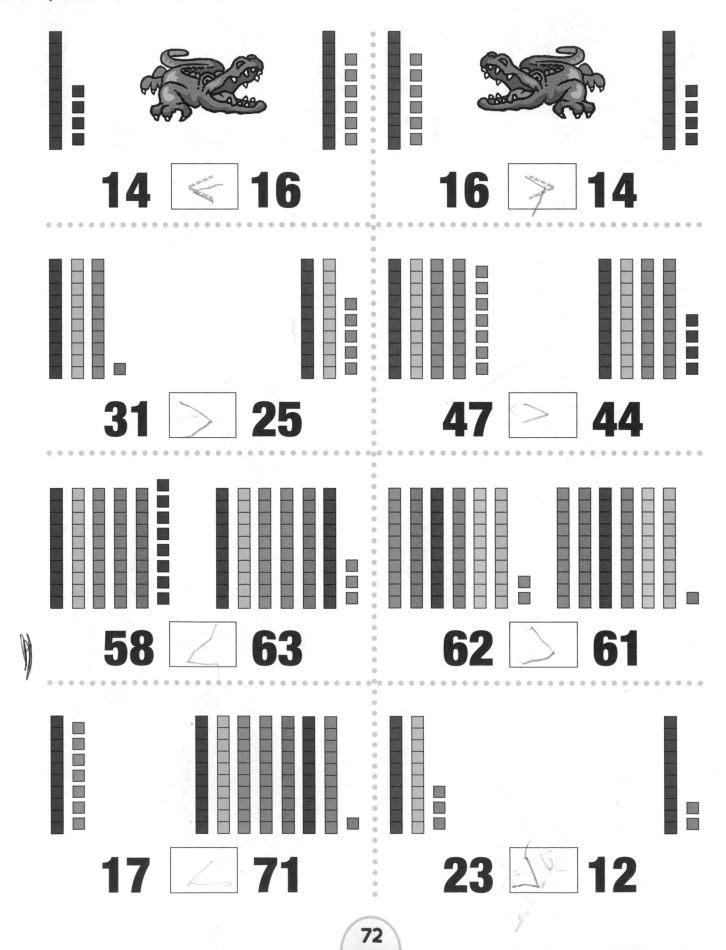

14 < 16

16 > 14

31 > 25

47 > 44

58 < 63

62 > 61

17 < 71

23 > 12

Compare the numbers. Then write >, <, or = in each box.

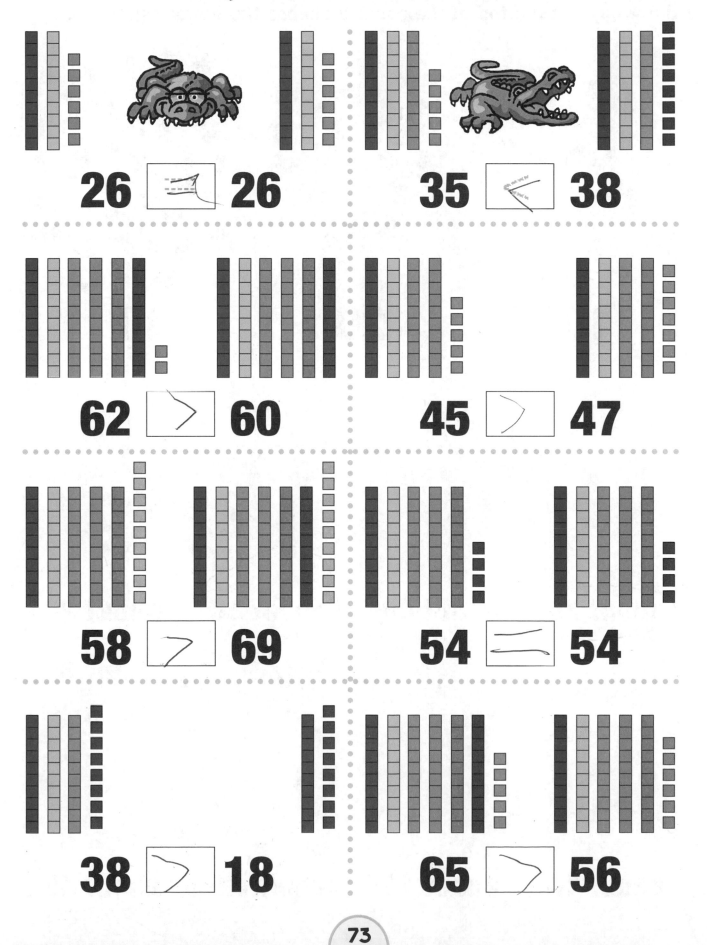

26 [=] 26

35 [<] 38

62 [>] 60

45 [<] 47

58 [>] 69

54 [=] 54

38 [>] 18

65 [>] 56

Using Estimation

Write how many tens and ones.
Use the groups at the top of the page to choose the better estimates.

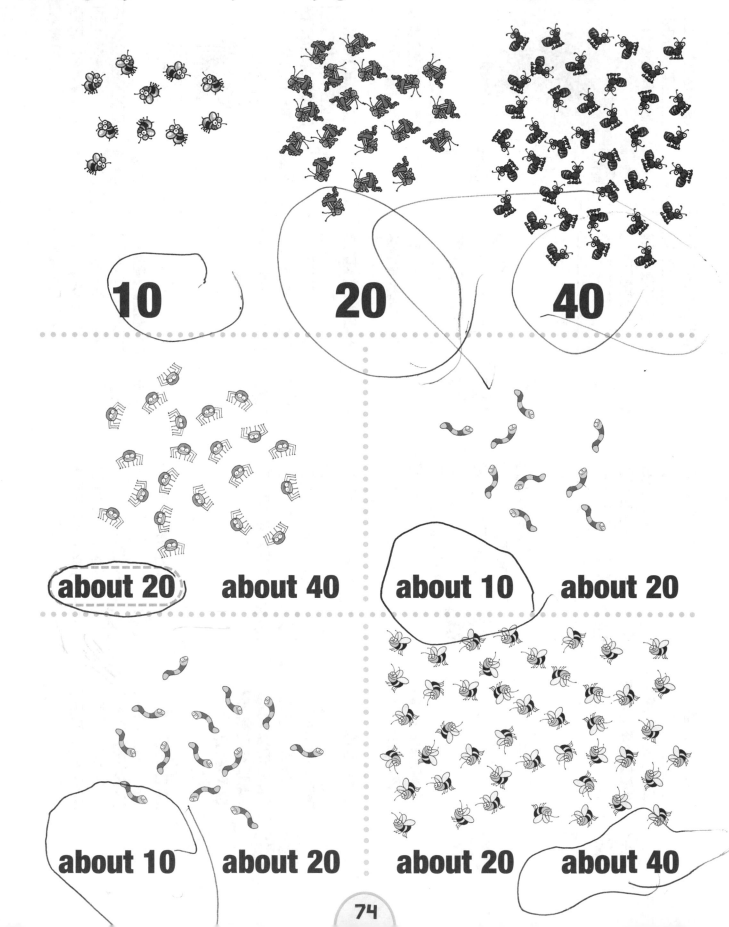

10   **20**   **40**

about 20   about 40   about 10   about 20

about 10   about 20   about 20   about 40

Using Estimation

Draw a line from each number to its most reasonable estimate.

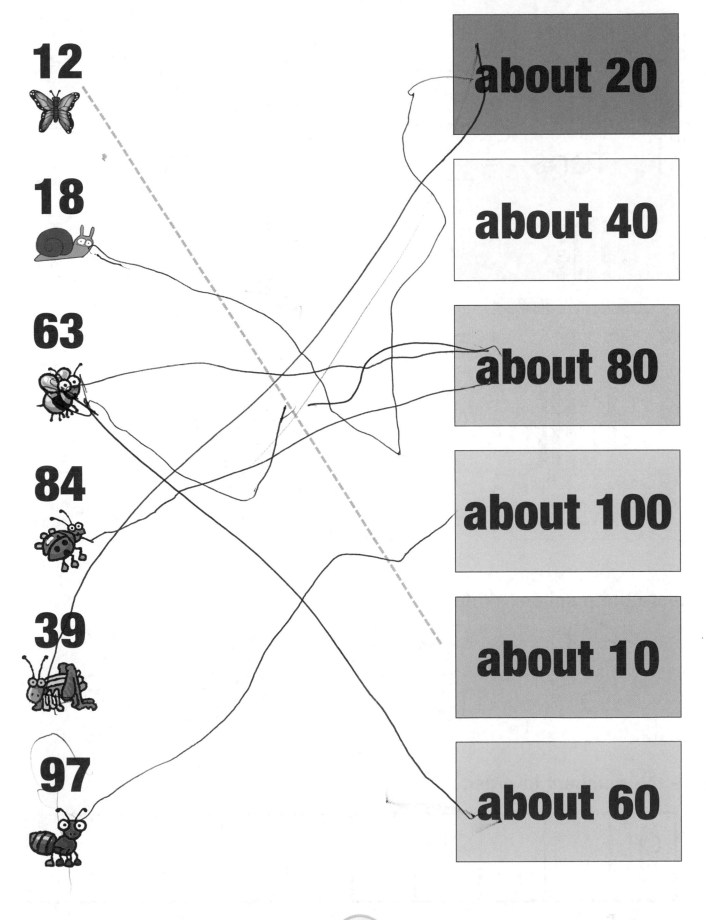

12

18

63

84

39

97

about 20

about 40

about 80

about 100

about 10

about 60

Write each number.

10 + 3 = _____   10 + ___ = 15

80 + 10 = _____   50 + 10 = _____

4 tens = _____   7 tens = _____

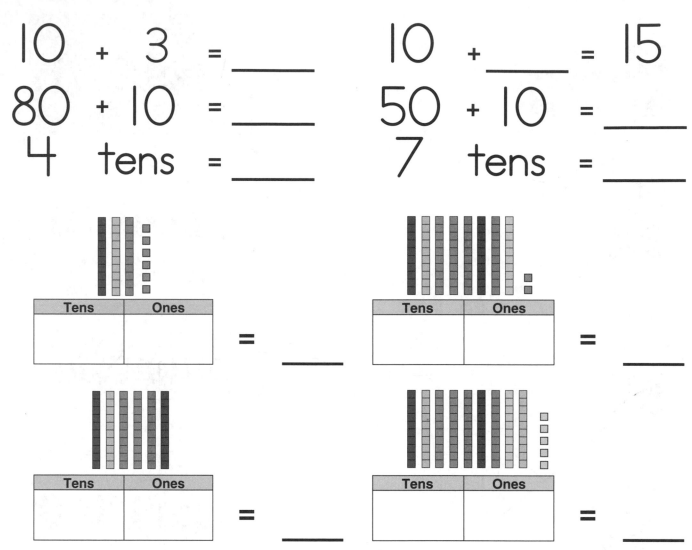

Tens	Ones

= _____

Tens	Ones

= _____

Tens	Ones

= _____

Tens	Ones

= _____

Compare the numbers. Write >, <, or = in each box.

69 ☐ 99   35 ☐ 37

15 ☐ 15   88 ☐ 78

Write the numbers in order.

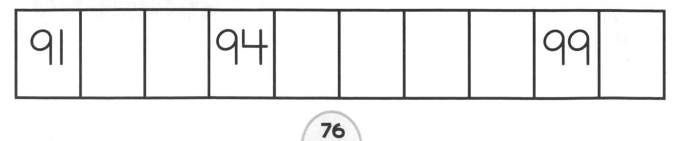

| 91 | | | 94 | | | | | 99 | |

Guess to the nearest ten. Then count and write how many in each group.

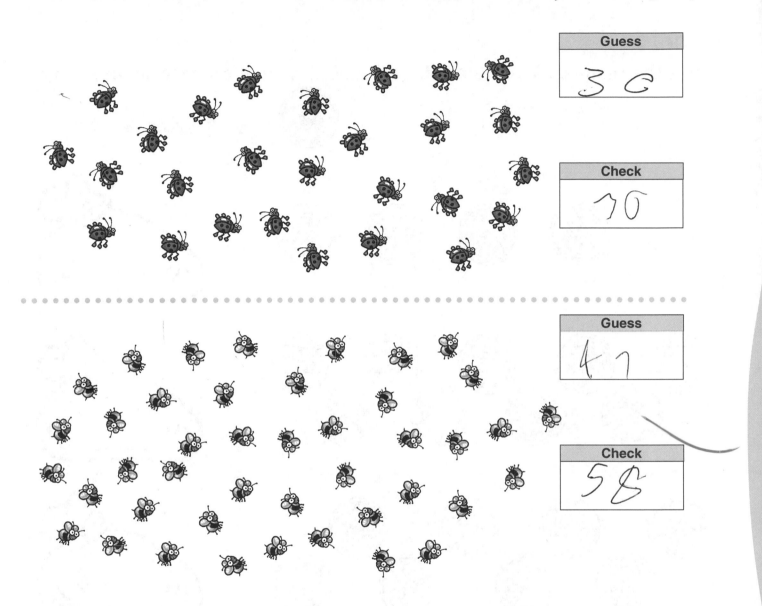

Guess
3 6

Check
70

Guess
4 7

Check
5 8

Choose the best estimate for the group of grasshoppers.

about 20   about 40

Pennies

Count the pennies. Write the total amount of money on each money bag.

 = 1 cent = 1¢

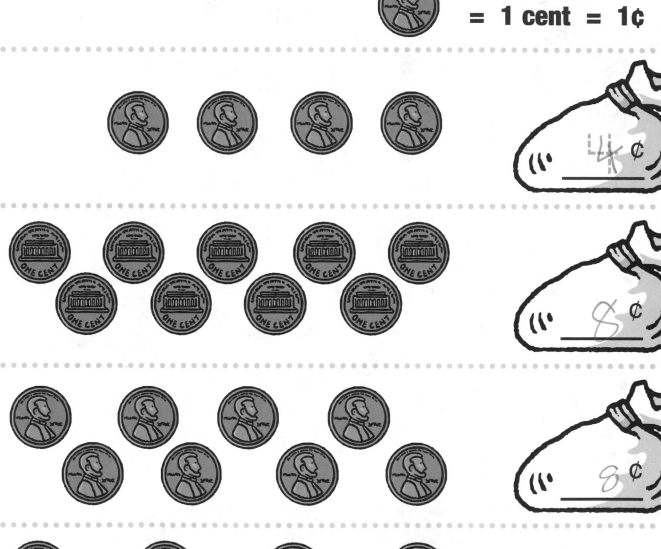

4 ¢

8 ¢

8 ¢

22 ¢

Pennies

Circle the number of pennies needed to buy each item.

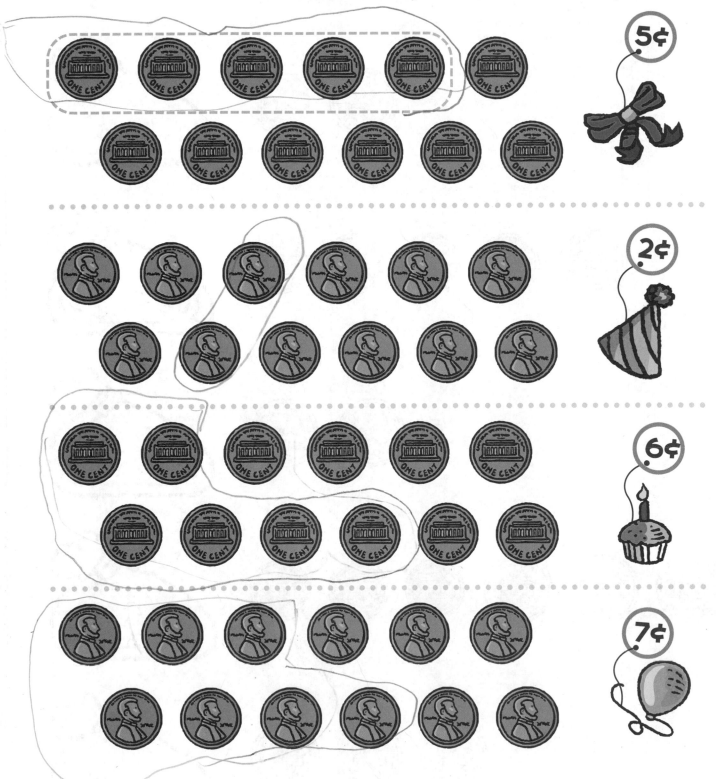

Nickels and Pennies

Count the pennies and nickels.
Write the total amount of money on each money bag.

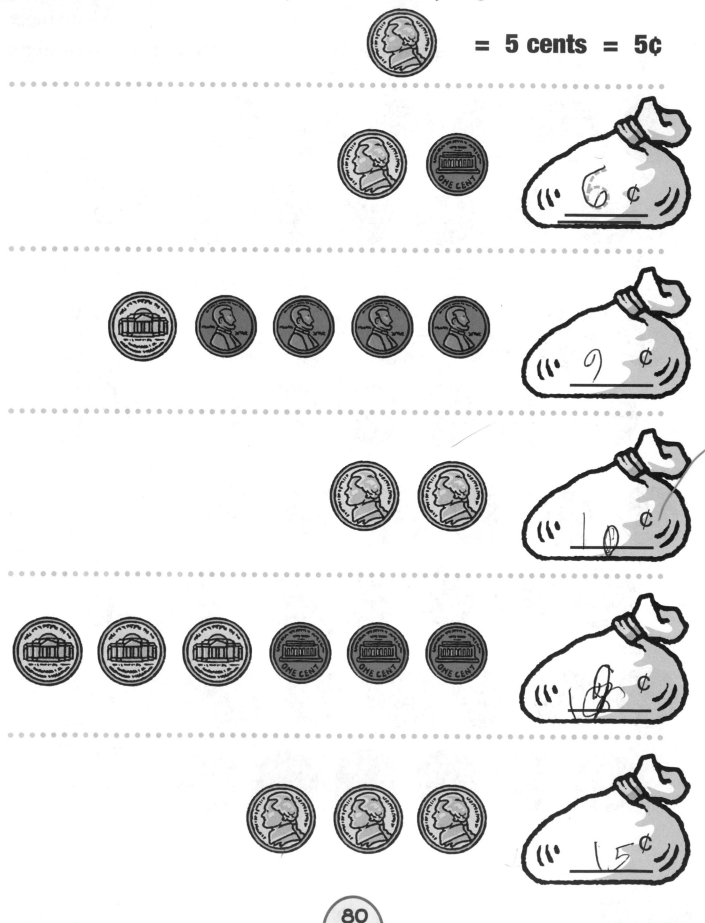

= 5 cents = 5¢

6 ¢

9 ¢

| ¢

¢

5¢

Nickels and Pennies

Draw a line from each item to the coins needed to buy it.

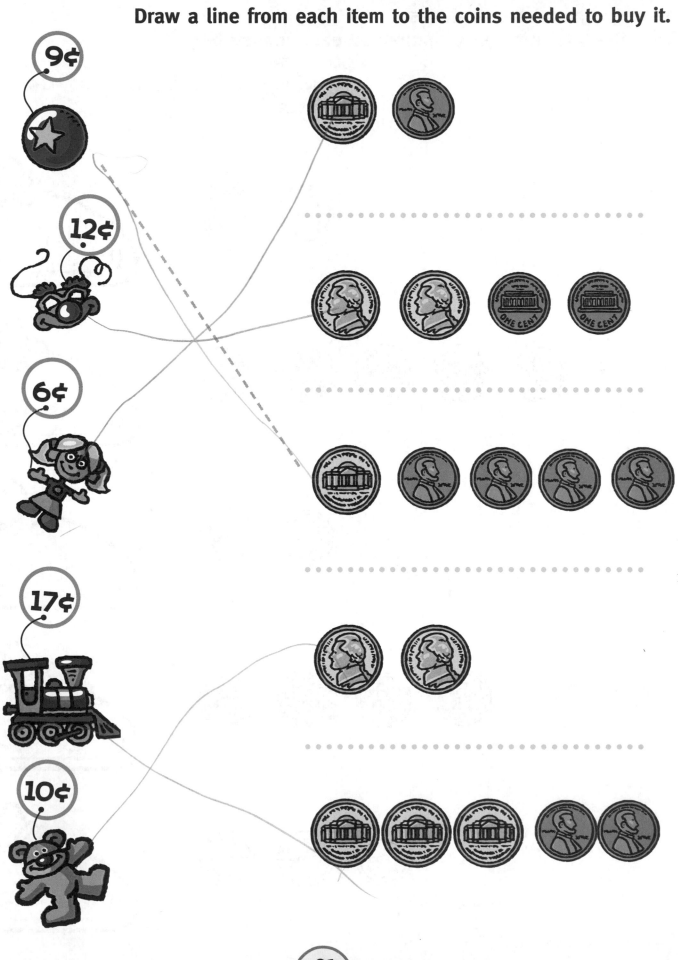

Dimes and Pennies

Count the pennies and dimes.
Write the total amount of money on each money bag.

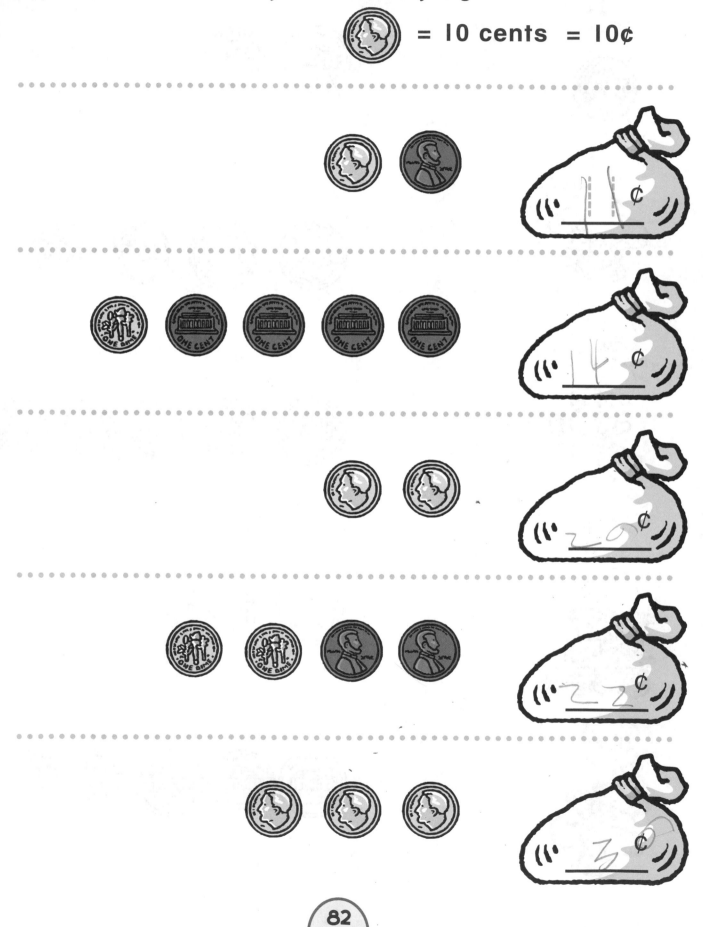

= 10 cents = 10¢

Dimes and Pennies

Draw a line from each item to the coins needed to buy it.

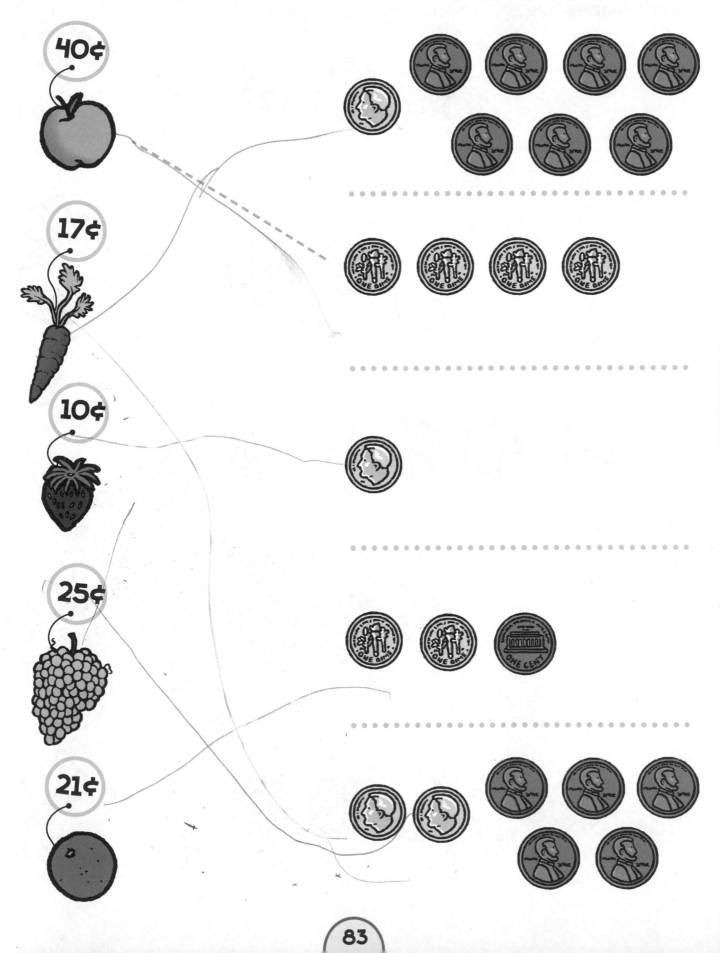

Pennies, Nickels, and Dimes

Count the pennies, nickels, and dimes. Write the total amount of money on each money bag.

Pennies, Nickels, and Dimes

Draw a line from each item to the coins needed to buy it.

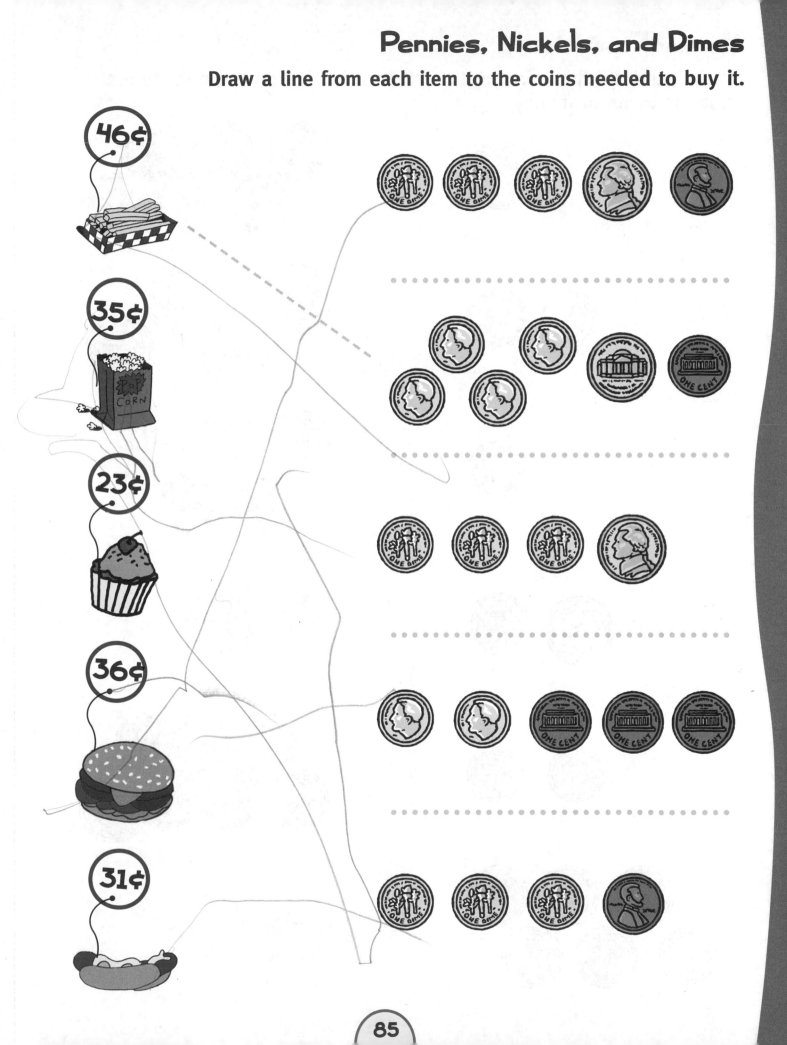

Money Equivalents

Draw lines from the coins on the left to the coins on the right to match equal amounts of money.

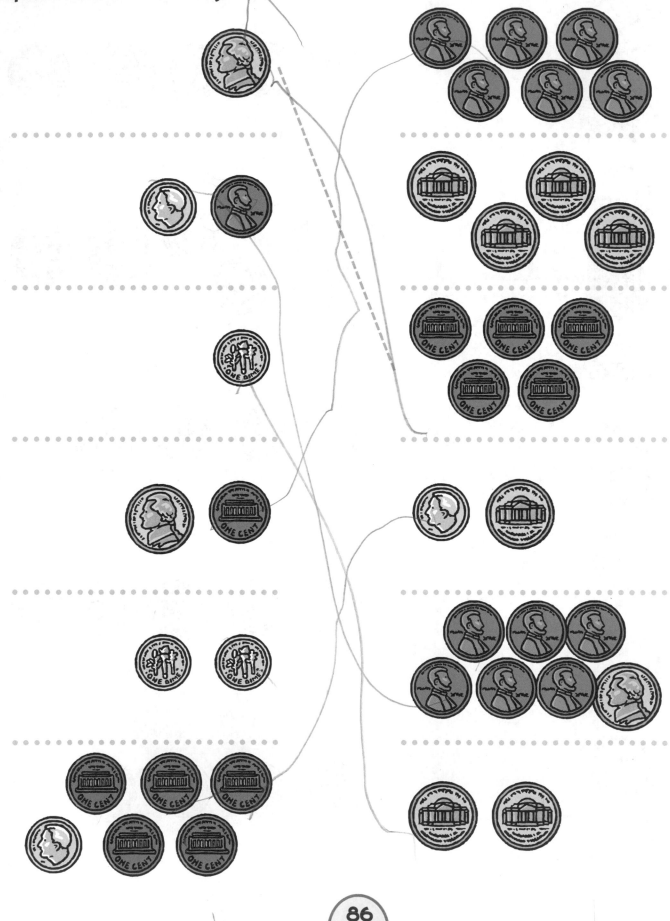

Money Equivalents

Count each group of coins and write the amounts.
Then draw lines to match equal amounts of money.

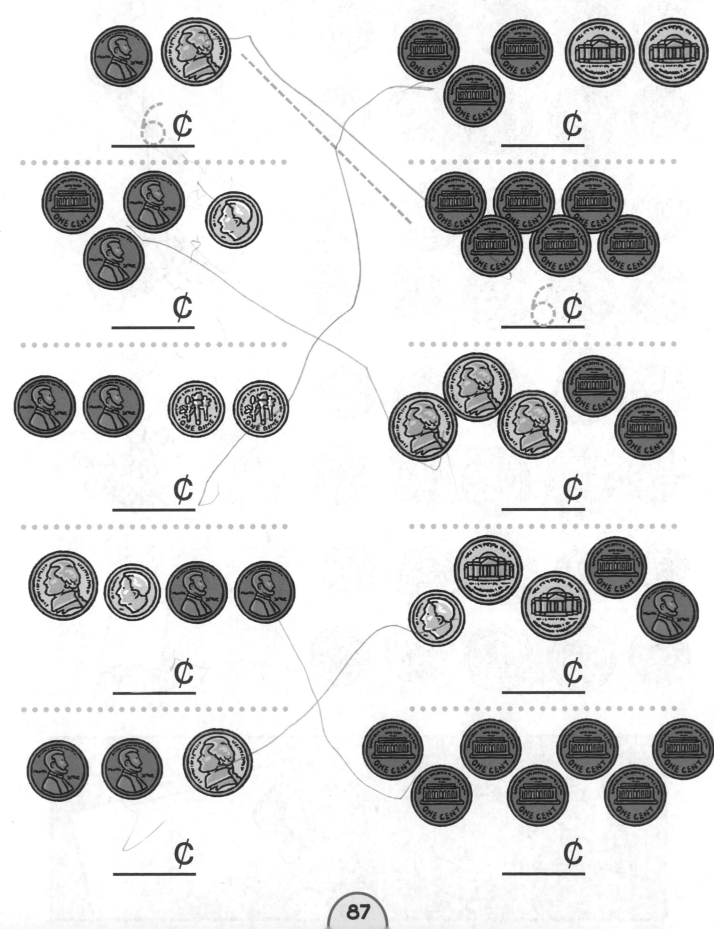

_____ ¢

_____ ¢

_____ ¢

_____ ¢

_____ ¢

_____ ¢

_____ ¢

_____ ¢

_____ ¢

_____ ¢

Show How Much

Circle the coins needed to buy each item.

13¢

14¢

20¢

35¢

Circle the coins needed to buy each item.

30¢

31¢

6¢

ABC DEF GHI

22¢

40¢

INK

89

Using Logic

Count how much money is in each group of coins.
Then draw how much more money you need to buy each item.

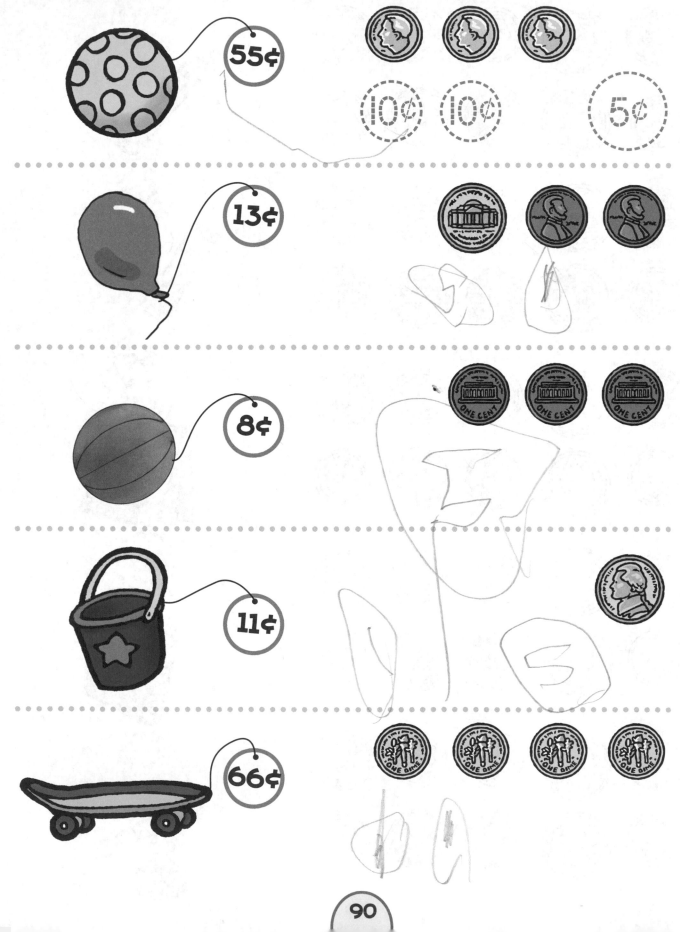

Count how much money is in each group of coins.
Then draw how much more money you need to buy each item.

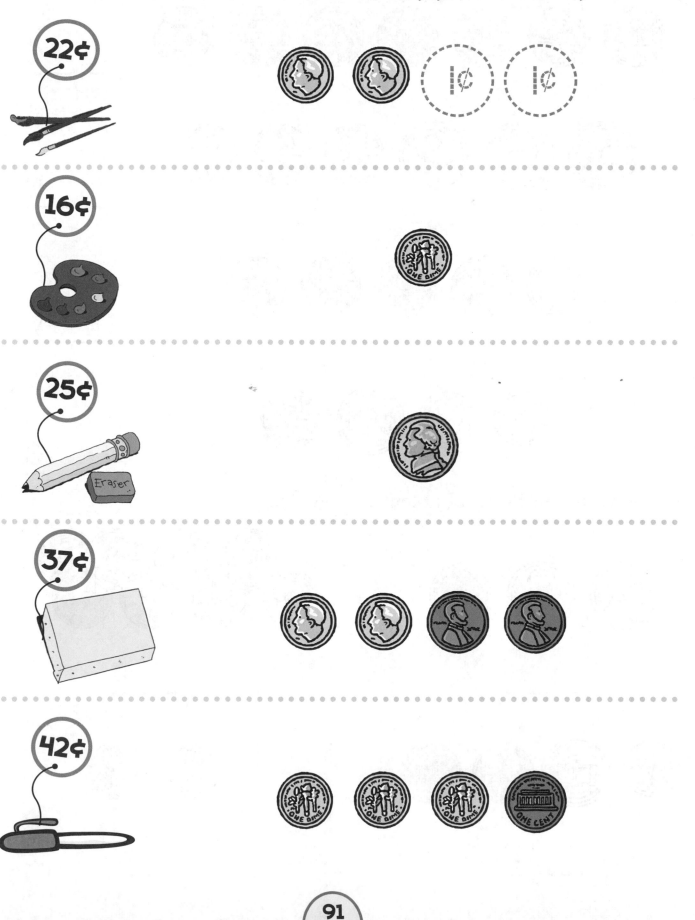

Unit 5 Review

Write the total amount of money for each group of coins.

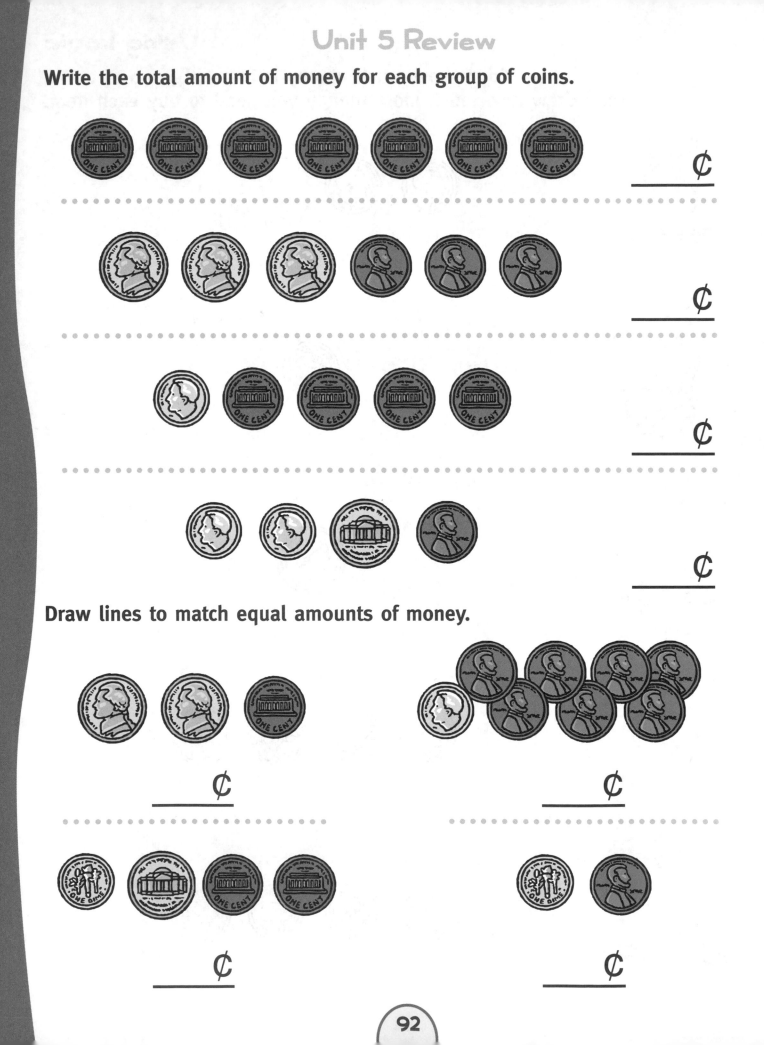

_____ ¢

_____ ¢

_____ ¢

_____ ¢

Draw lines to match equal amounts of money.

_____ ¢   _____ ¢

_____ ¢   _____ ¢

Draw the coins needed to buy each item.

Draw the coins that are missing.

Parts of a Clock

Color the face yellow, the hour hand pink, and the minute hand blue.
Then circle the number where the hour hand points.

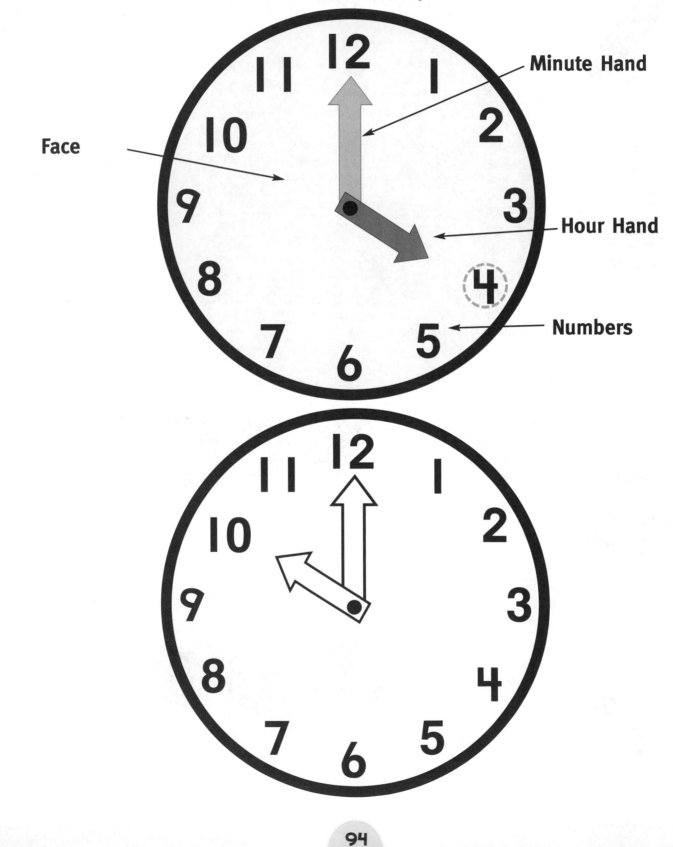

Minute Hand

Face

Hour Hand

Numbers

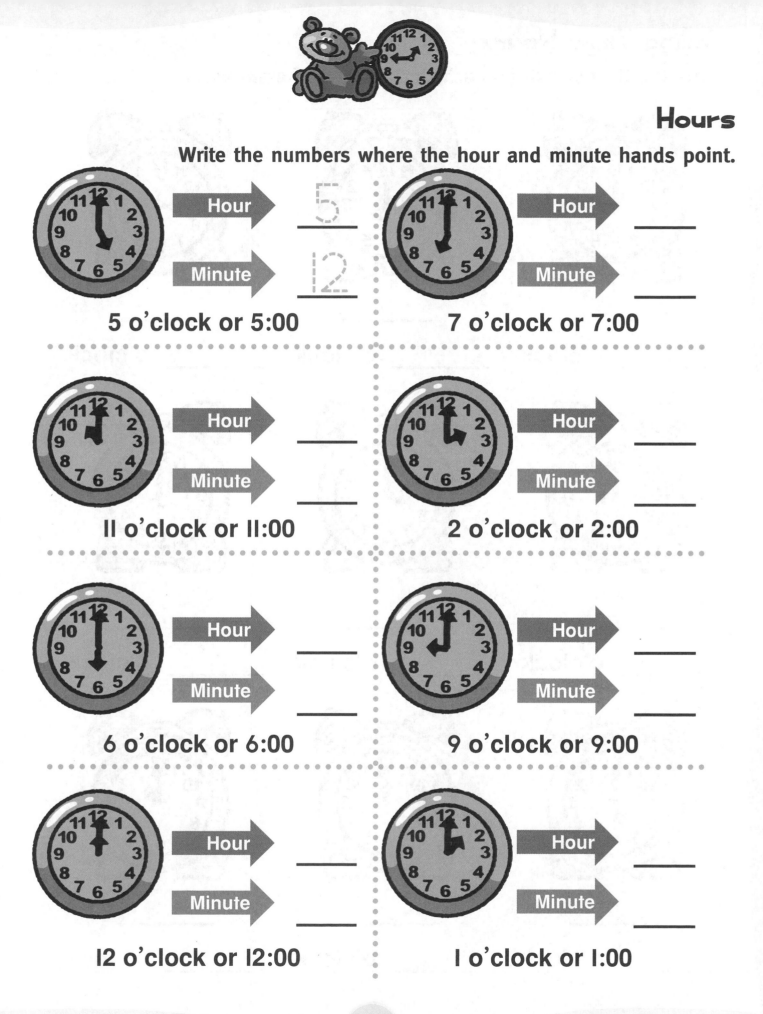

Write the numbers where the hour and minute hands point.

Hour ➤ 5

Minute ➤ 12

5 o'clock or 5:00

Hour ➤ _____

Minute ➤ _____

7 o'clock or 7:00

Hour ➤ _____

Minute ➤ _____

11 o'clock or 11:00

Hour ➤ _____

Minute ➤ _____

2 o'clock or 2:00

Hour ➤ _____

Minute ➤ _____

6 o'clock or 6:00

Hour ➤ _____

Minute ➤ _____

9 o'clock or 9:00

Hour ➤ _____

Minute ➤ _____

12 o'clock or 12:00

Hour ➤ _____

Minute ➤ _____

1 o'clock or 1:00

Telling Time: Hours

Write the time shown on each clock in two different ways.

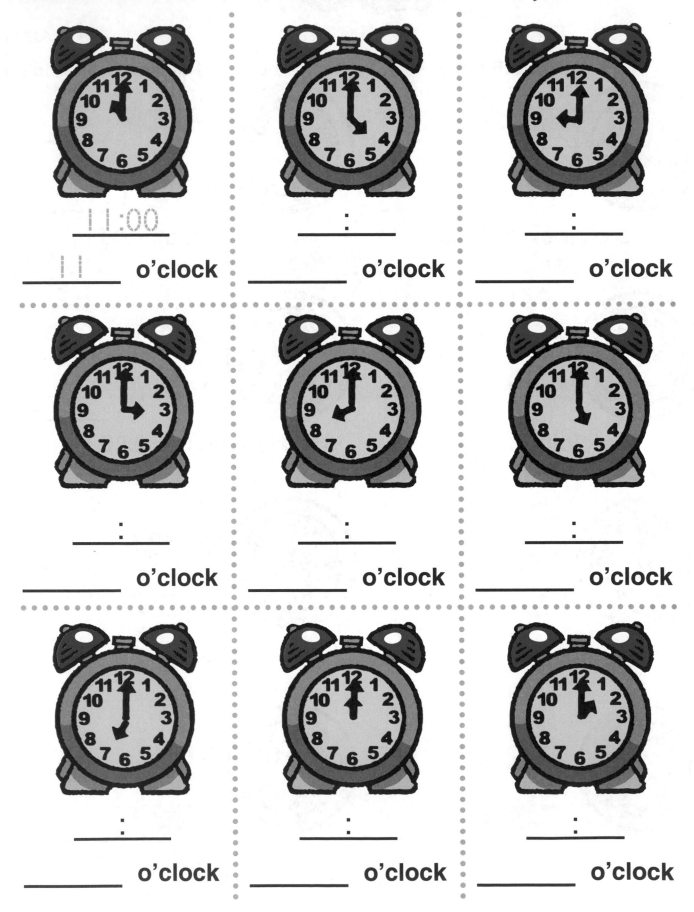

_11:00_

_11_ o'clock

___:___

_____ o'clock

___:___

_____ o'clock

___:___

_____ o'clock

___:___

_____ o'clock

___:___

_____ o'clock

___:___

_____ o'clock

___:___

_____ o'clock

___:___

_____ o'clock

Write the times on the digital clocks to match the first clock in each pair.

Telling Time: Hours

Draw an hour hand on each clock to show the time.

Complete a Pattern

Draw hands on the clocks to show the next time in each pattern.

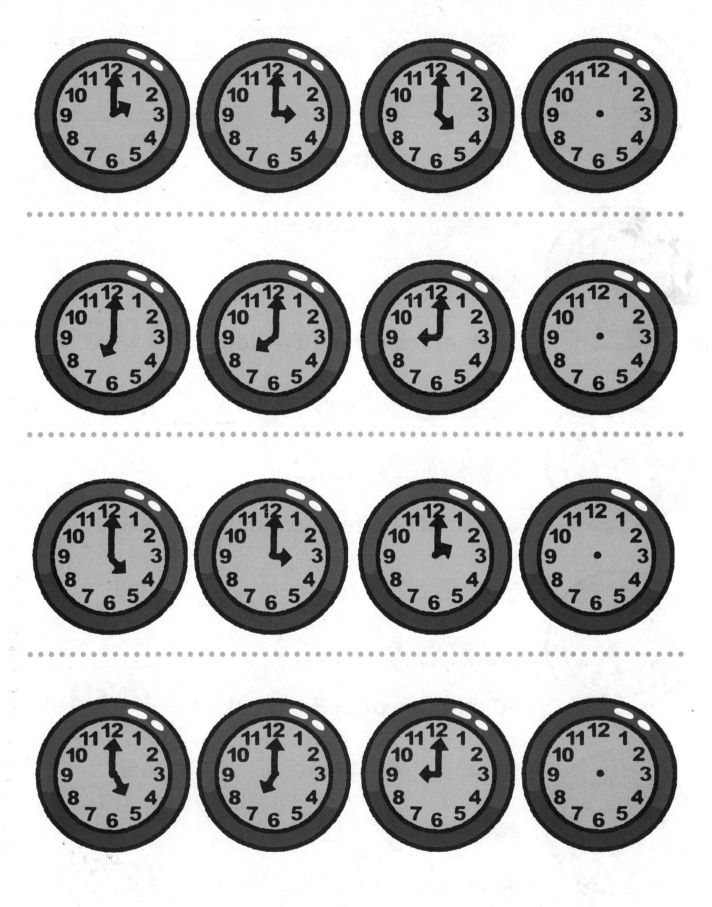

Half Hours

Write where the hour and minute hands point.

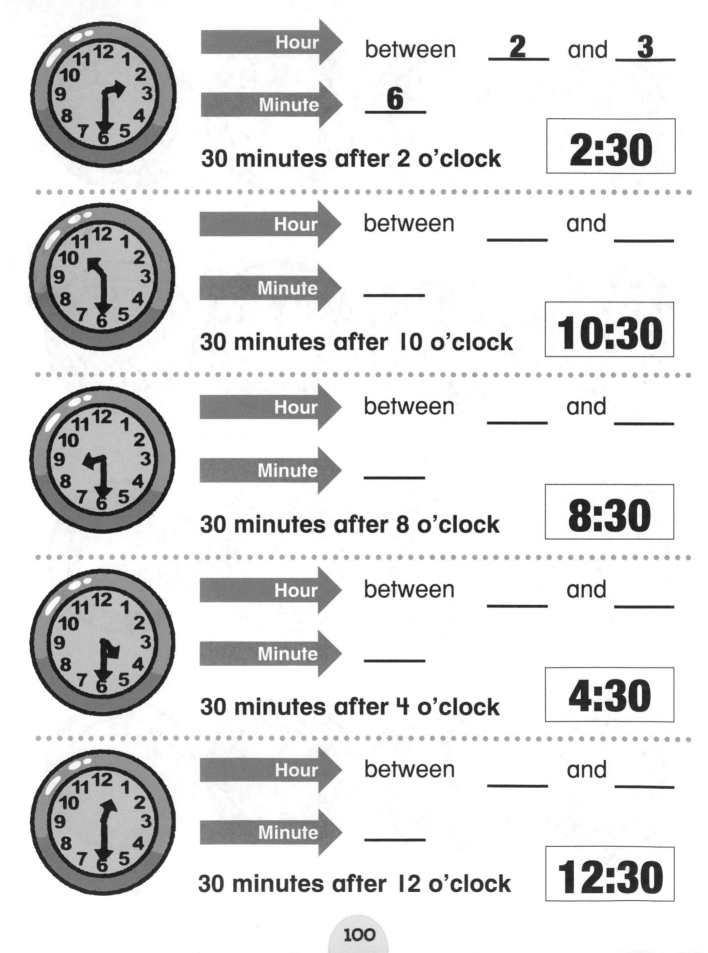

Hour → between __2__ and __3__

Minute → __6__

30 minutes after 2 o'clock

2:30

Hour → between ___ and ___

Minute → ___

30 minutes after 10 o'clock

10:30

Hour → between ___ and ___

Minute → ___

30 minutes after 8 o'clock

8:30

Hour → between ___ and ___

Minute → ___

30 minutes after 4 o'clock

4:30

Hour → between ___ and ___

Minute → ___

30 minutes after 12 o'clock

12:30

Write where the hour and minute hands point.

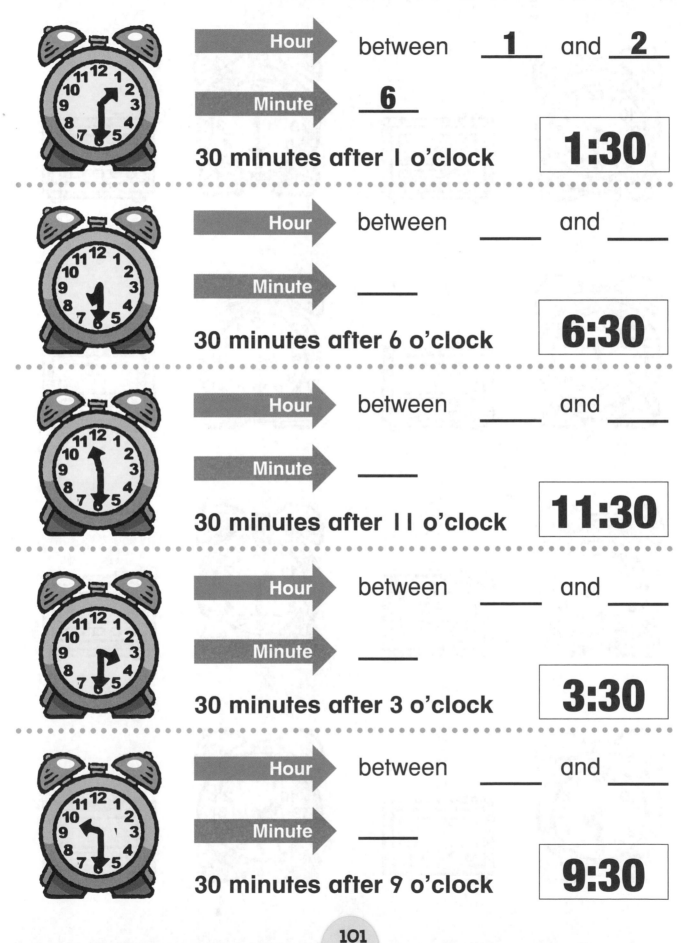

Hour → between ___1___ and ___2___

Minute → ___6___

30 minutes after 1 o'clock

1:30

Hour → between ___ and ___

Minute → ___

30 minutes after 6 o'clock

6:30

Hour → between ___ and ___

Minute → ___

30 minutes after 11 o'clock

11:30

Hour → between ___ and ___

Minute → ___

30 minutes after 3 o'clock

3:30

Hour → between ___ and ___

Minute → ___

30 minutes after 9 o'clock

9:30

Telling Time: Half Hours

Write the times on the digital clocks to match the first clock in each pair.

Telling Time: Half Hours

Draw a line between the clocks that show the same time.

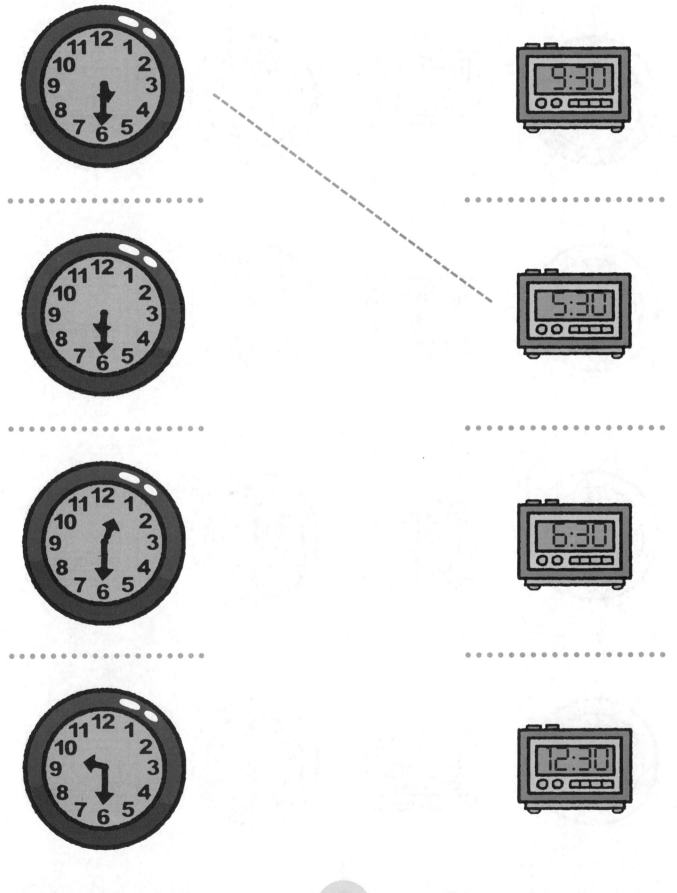

Using Logic

Look at the time shown on the first clock.
Then write the time that shows one hour later on the digital clock.

Look at the time shown on the first clock.
Then write the time that shows one half hour later on the digital clock.

105

Unit 6 Review

Write the time shown on each clock.

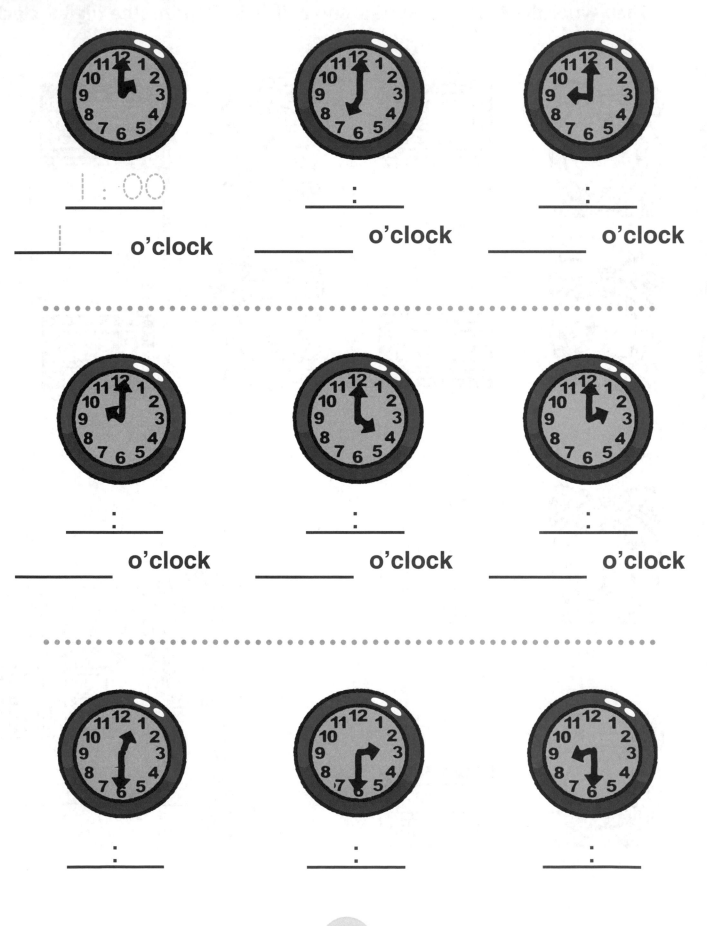

1 : 00

_____1_____ o'clock

____ : ____

_____ o'clock

____ : ____

_____ o'clock

____ : ____

_____ o'clock

____ : ____

_____ o'clock

____ : ____

_____ o'clock

____ : ____

____ : ____

____ : ____

Unit 6 Review

Write the next time to complete each pattern.

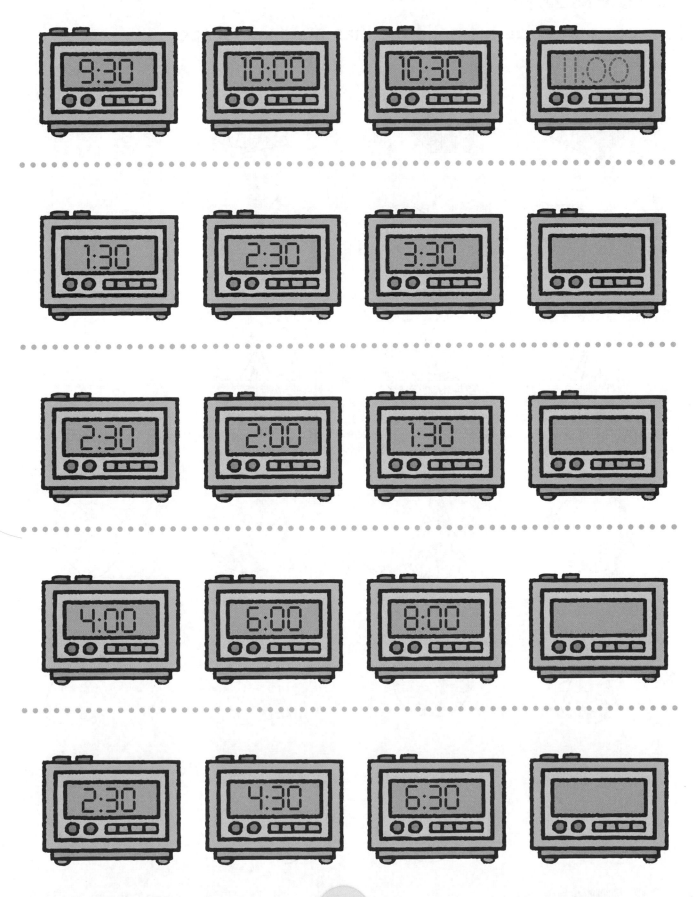

9:30 10:00 10:30 11:00

1:30 2:30 3:30 ____

2:30 2:00 1:30 ____

4:00 6:00 8:00 ____

2:30 4:30 6:30 ____

Solid Figures

For each row, circle the solid that has the same shape.

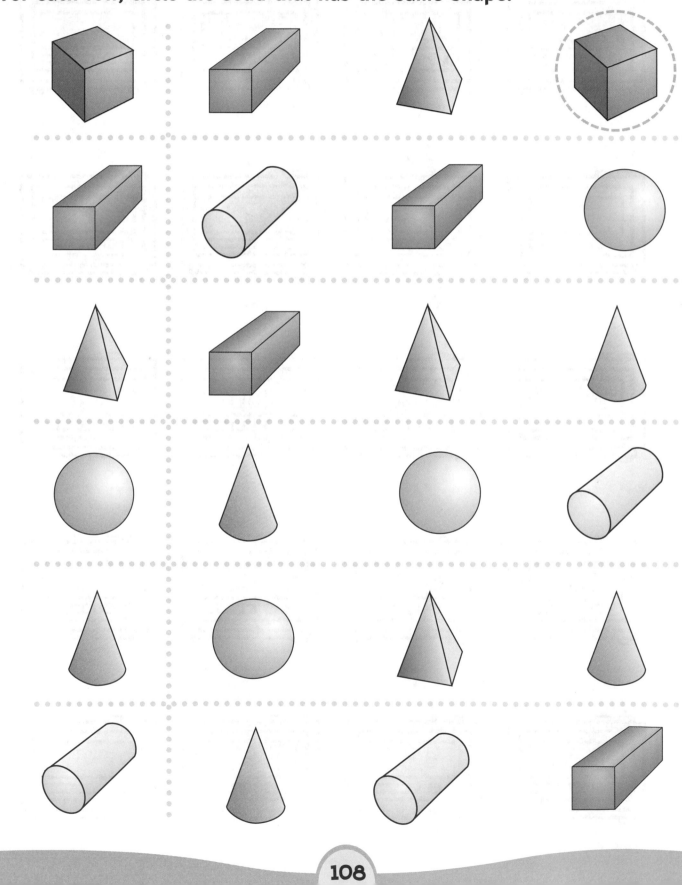

Solid Figures

Draw a line between the solids that have the same shape.

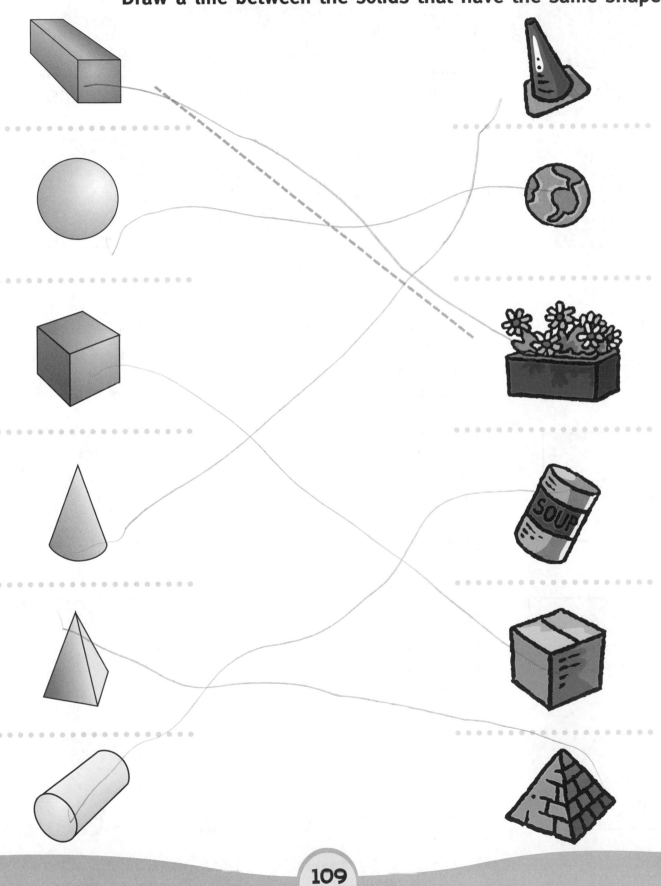

Plane Figures

In each row, mark the figure that is the same shape as the first.

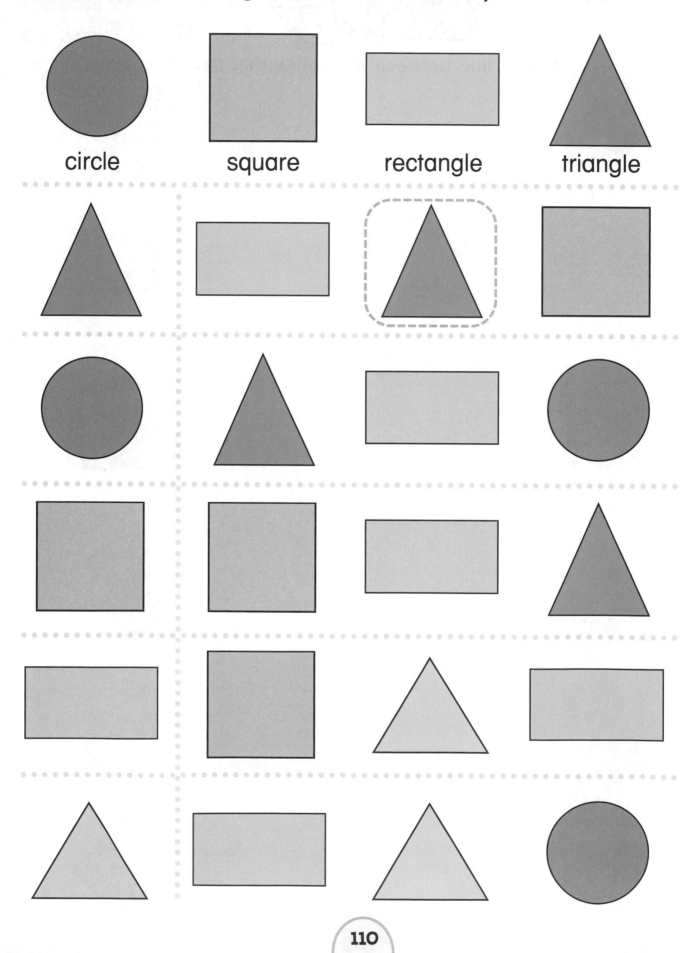

circle   square   rectangle   triangle

Write the name of the shape for each picture.

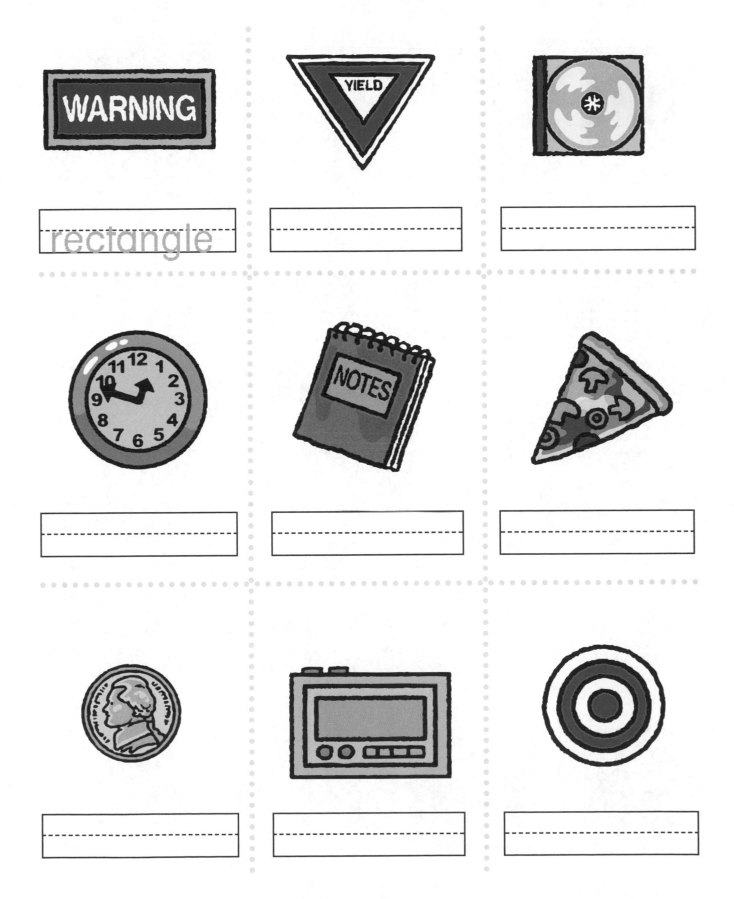

rectangle

Congruence

Draw a shape to match each one shown.

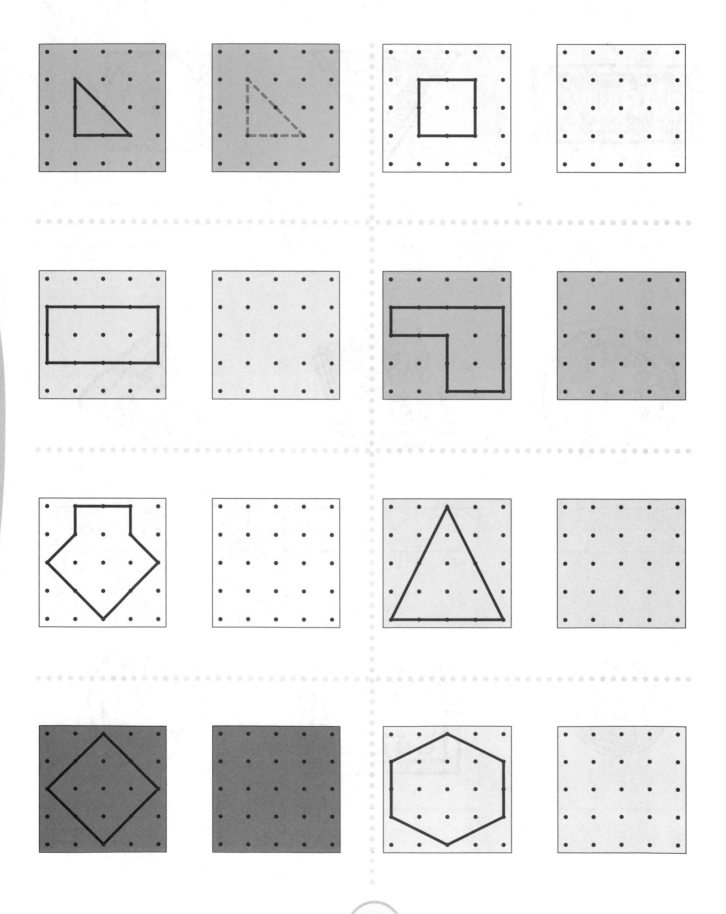

Symmetry

Draw the other half of each shape.

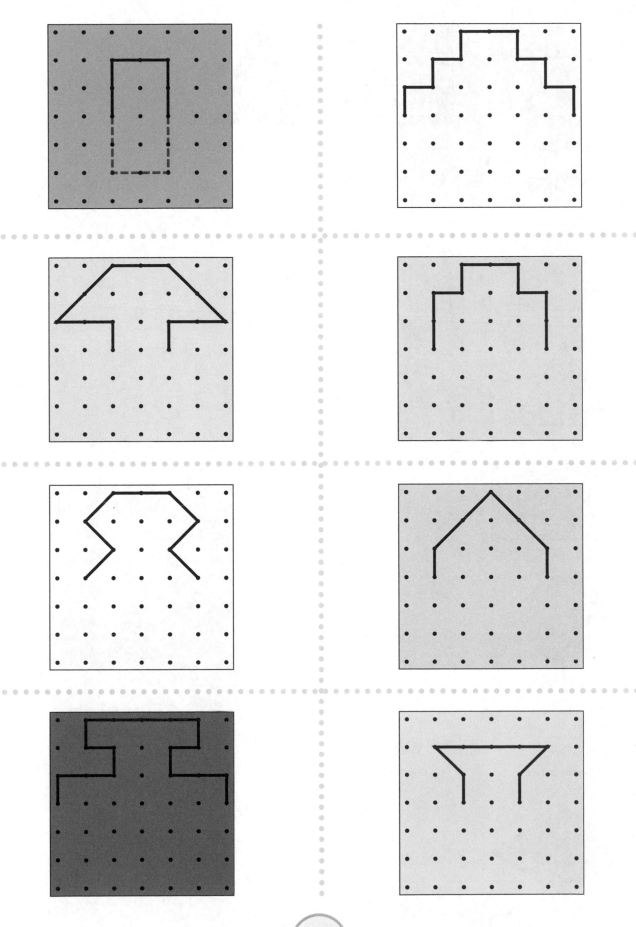

Using a Table

Write how many straight sides and corners each plane figure has.

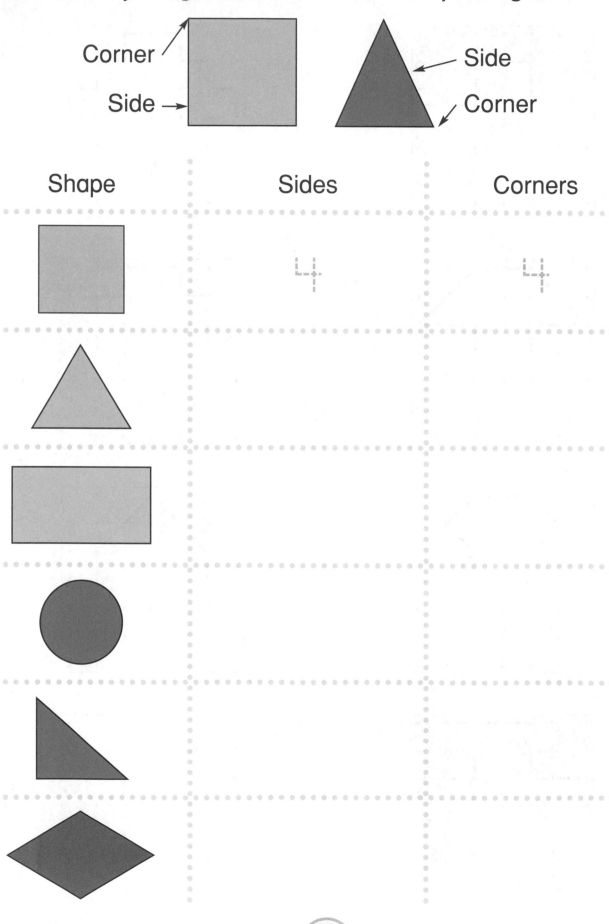

Shape	Sides	Corners
	4	4

Using a Table

Look at each solid to see if it has corners, faces, or curves.
Write yes or no in each box.

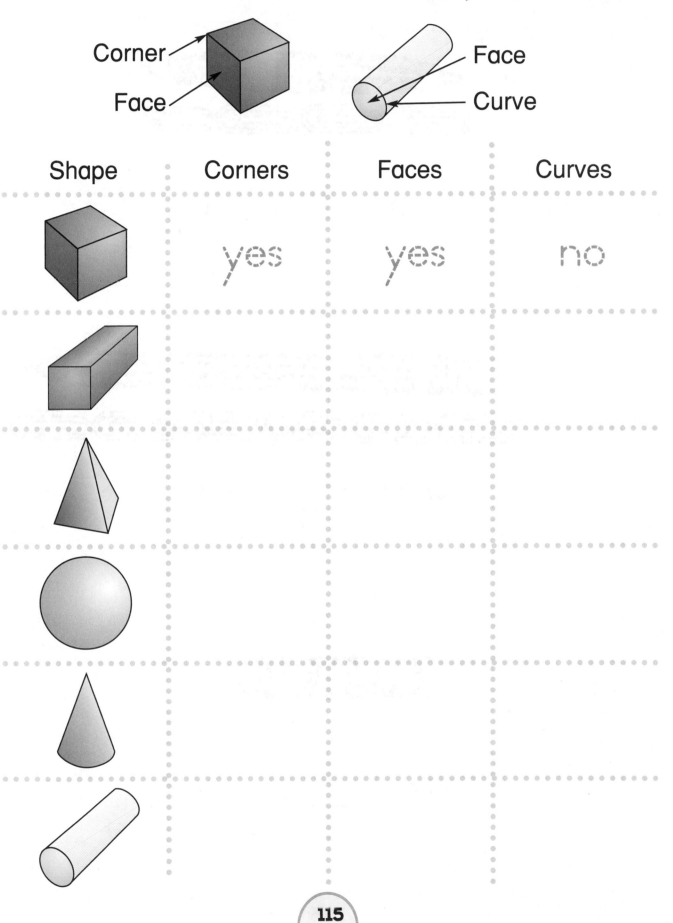

Shape	Corners	Faces	Curves
	yes	yes	no

Measuring: Nonstandard Units

Write the length of each object.

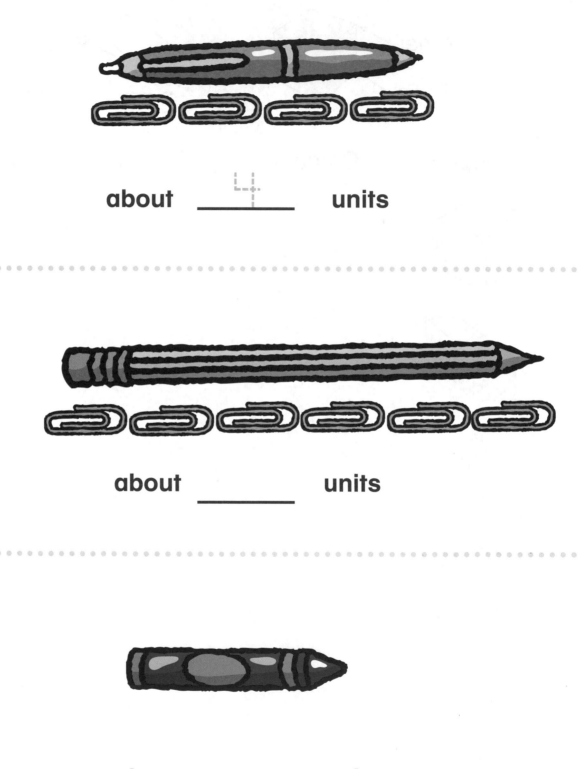

about ___4___ units

about _____ units

about _____ units

Write the length of each object.

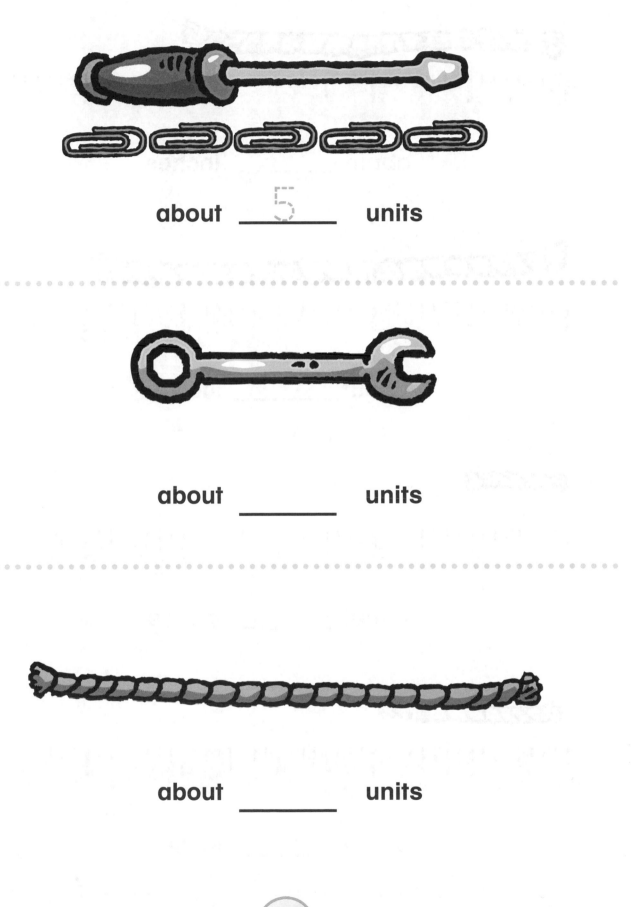

about ___5___ units

about _____ units

about _____ units

Measuring: Inches

Write the length of each object.

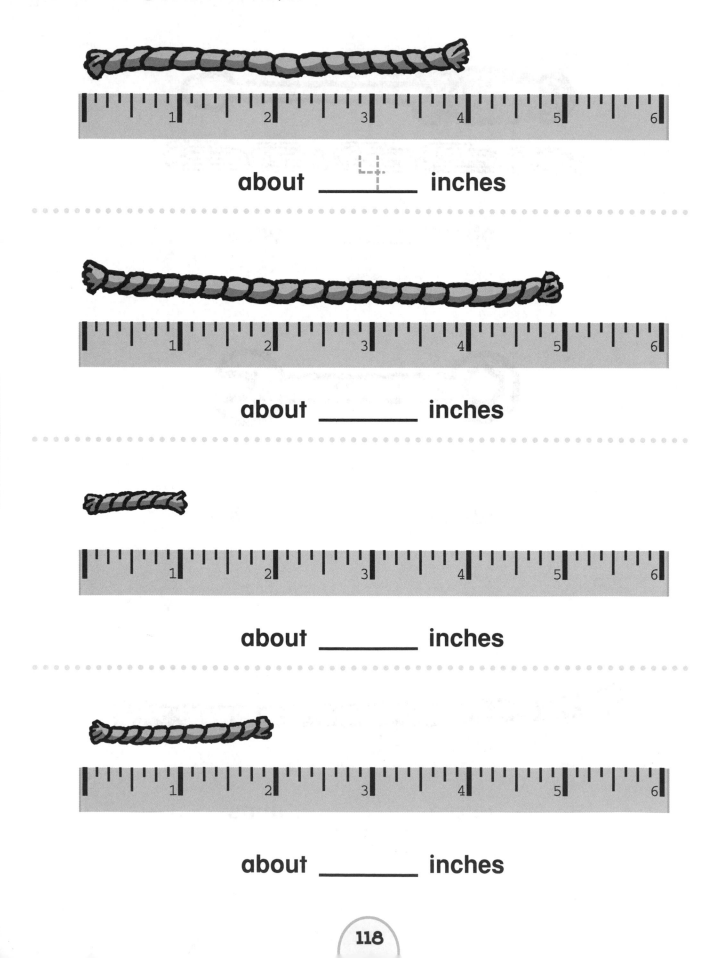

about _____4_____ inches

about _____ inches

about _____ inches

about _____ inches

Using an Inch Ruler

Use an inch ruler to measure each object.

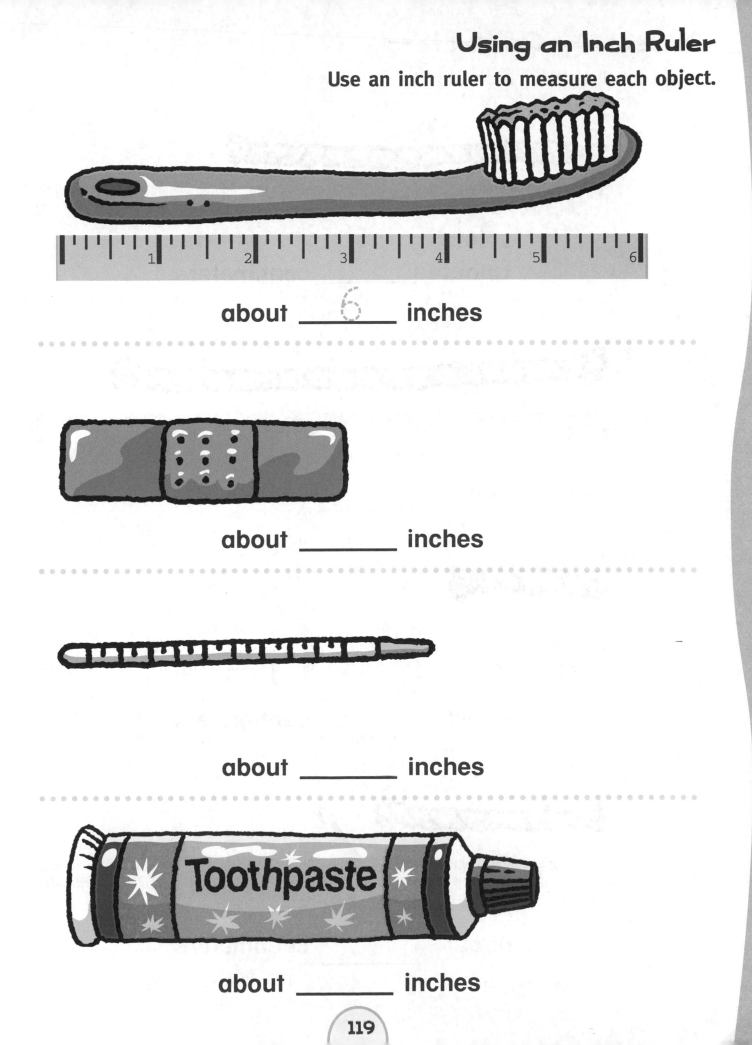

about _____6_____ inches

about _____ inches

about _____ inches

about _____ inches

Measuring: Centimeters

Write the length of each object.

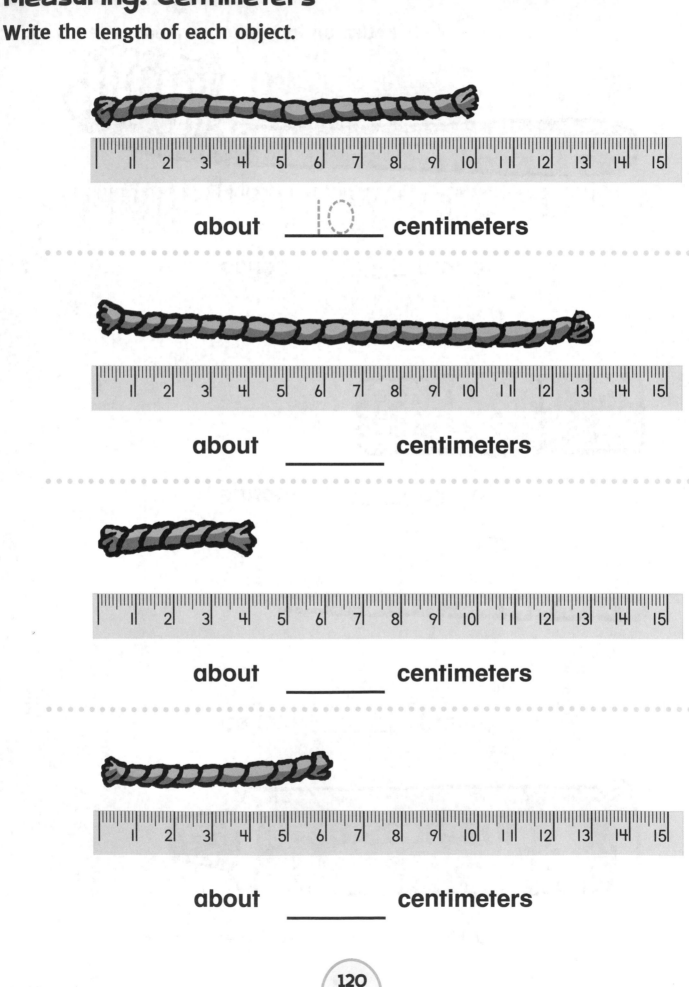

about ___10___ centimeters

about _____ centimeters

about _____ centimeters

about _____ centimeters

Use a centimeter ruler to measure each object.

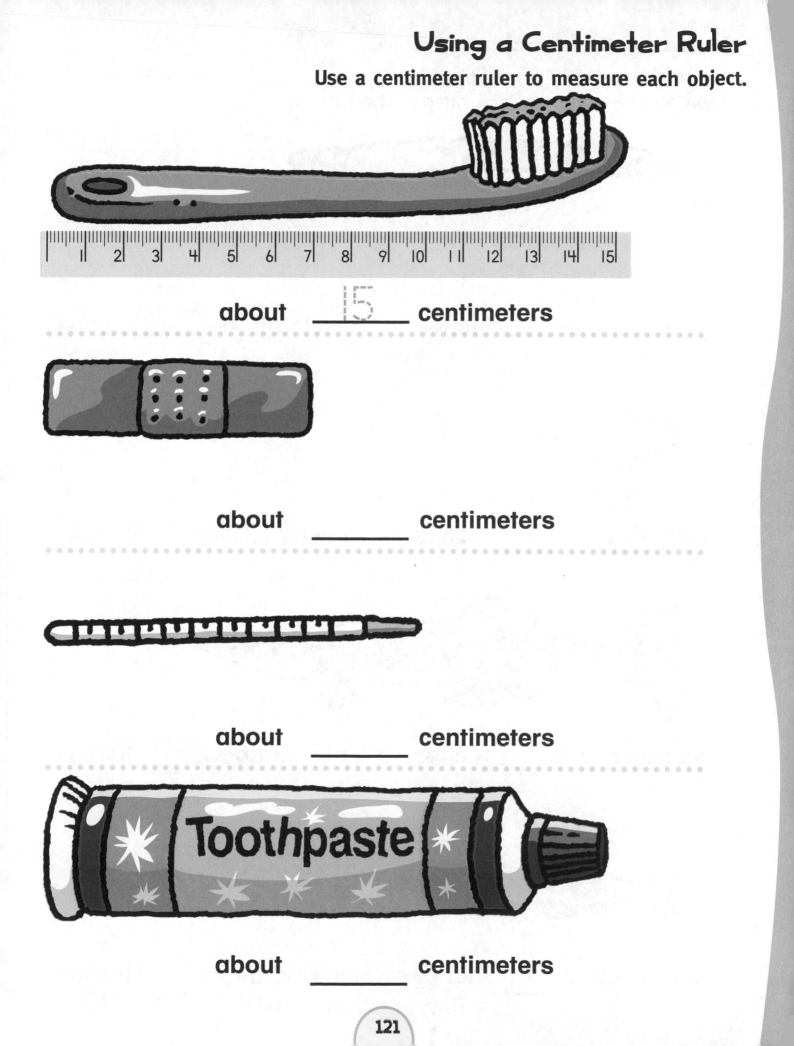

about ___15___ centimeters

about _____ centimeters

about _____ centimeters

about _____ centimeters

Guess and Check

Guess the length of each object.
Then measure with an inch ruler to check.

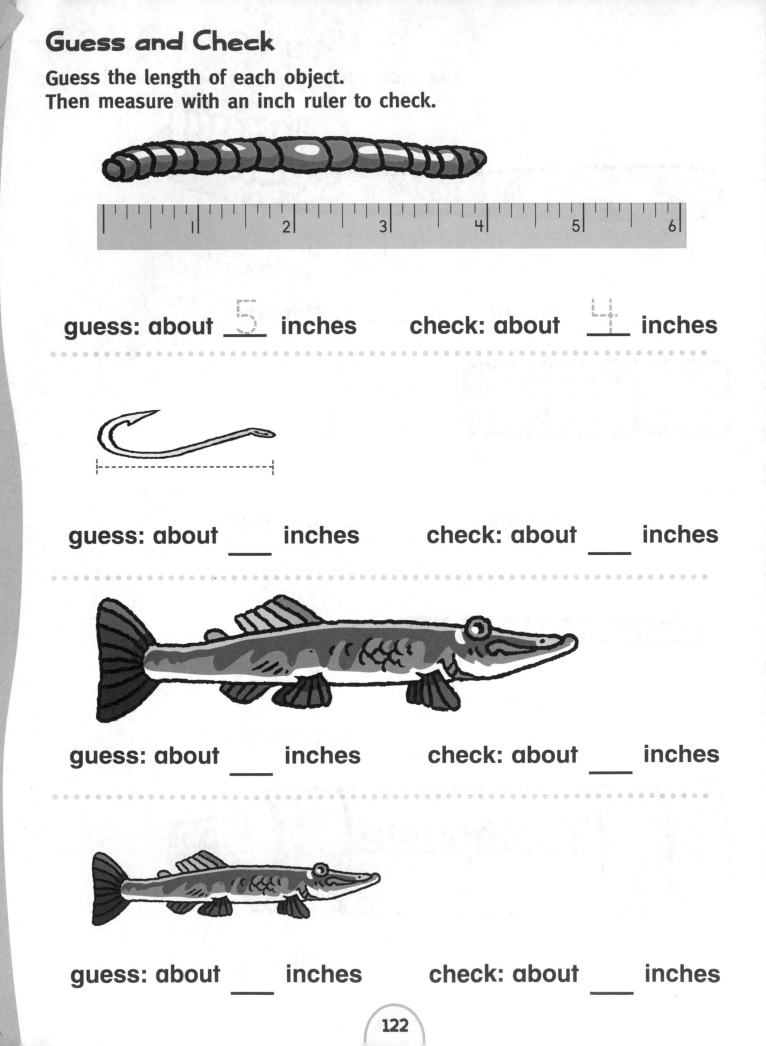

guess: about __5__ inches   check: about __4__ inches

guess: about ___ inches   check: about ___ inches

guess: about ___ inches   check: about ___ inches

guess: about ___ inches   check: about ___ inches

Guess and Check

Guess the length of each object.
Then measure with a centimeter ruler to check.

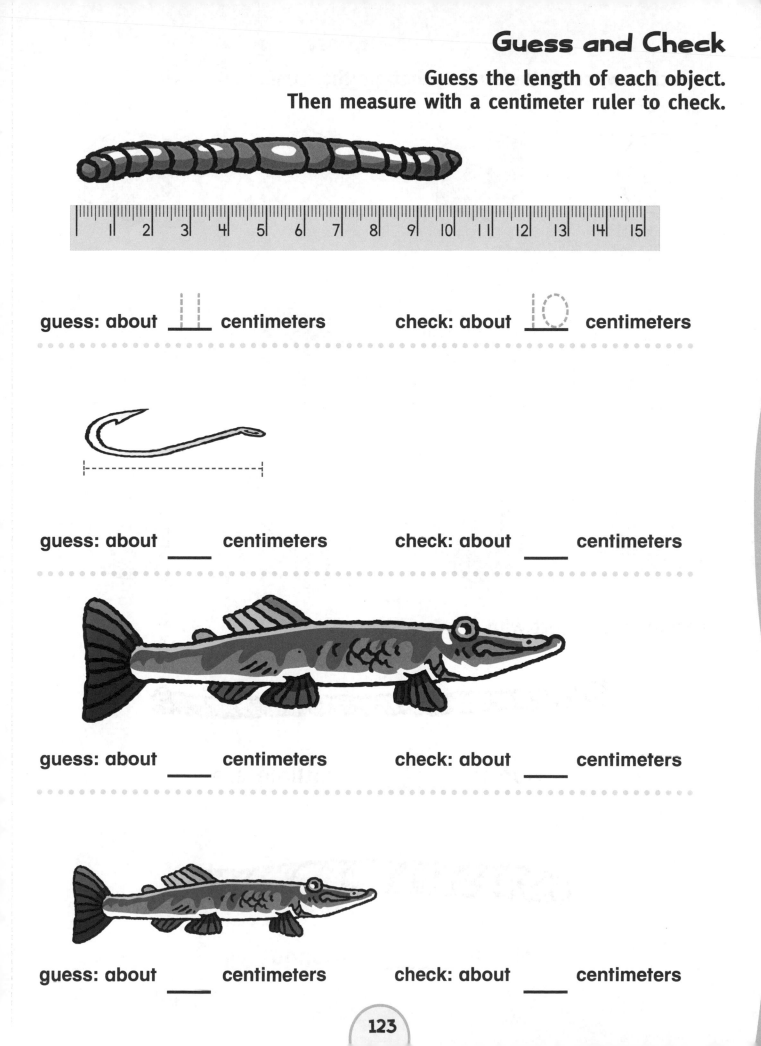

guess: about __11__ centimeters   check: about __10__ centimeters

guess: about ___ centimeters   check: about ___ centimeters

guess: about ___ centimeters   check: about ___ centimeters

guess: about ___ centimeters   check: about ___ centimeters

For each row, circle the shapes that are the same.

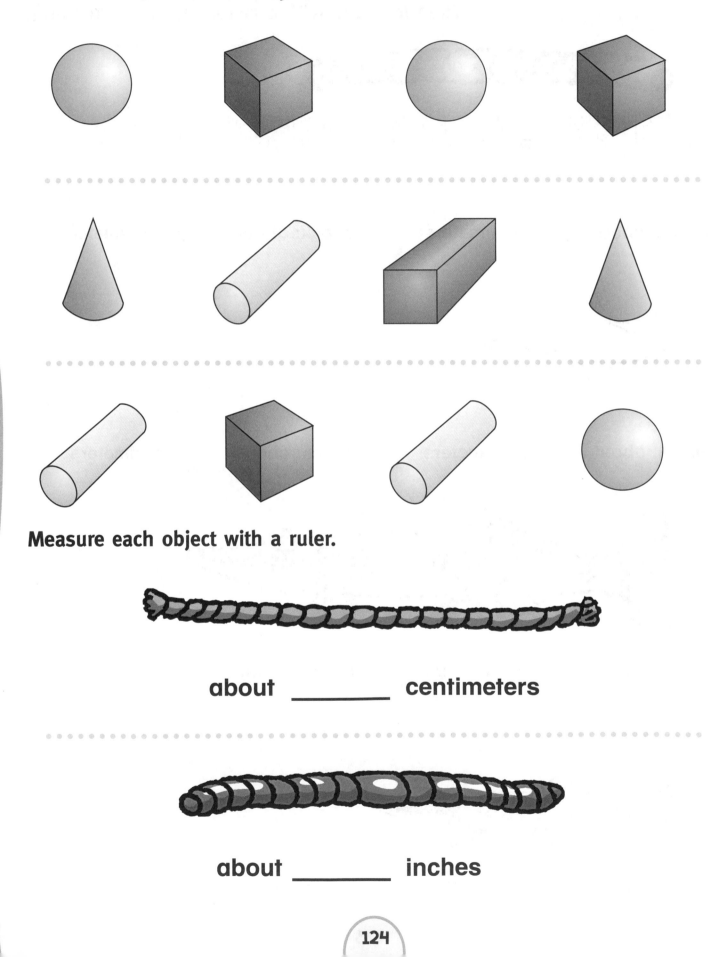

Measure each object with a ruler.

about _____ centimeters

about _____ inches

Guess how many inches long each object is.
Then measure with an inch ruler to check.

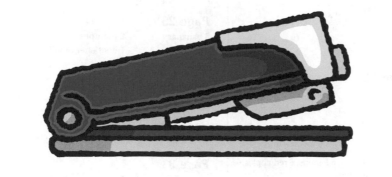

guess: about ___ inches   check: about ___ inches

guess: about ___ inches   check: about ___ inches

guess: about ___ inches   check: about ___ inches

Answer Key

Page 8

0	1	2	3	4	5
0	1	2	3	4	5

Page 9

3	2
0	1
5	4

Page 10

1	2	3	4	5
6	7	8	9	10

Page 11

5	6
2	7
9	1
4	10

Page 12

8	6
1	3
10	5
4	9
2	0

Page 13

1 lettuce, 2 grapes bunches, 3 watermelons, 4 carrots, 5 lemons, 6 red apples, 7 strawberries, 8 oranges, 9 green apples, and 10 bananas.

Page 14; after writing the numbers students should draw circles to show one more

4	5
2	3
9	10
7	8

Page 15

5   4
9   8
2   1
6   5

Page 16

0	1	2	5	6	7
7	8	9	2	3	4
3	4	5	1	2	3
6	7	8	8	9	10

Page 17

1	2	3
4	5	6
7	8	9

Page 18

1	2	3	4
3	4	5	6
5	6	7	8
2	3	4	5
7	8	9	10

Page 19

1	2	3	4	5				
1	2	3	4	5	6	7		
1	2	3	4	5	6	7	8	9
1	2	3	4					
1	2	3	4	5	6	7	8	9	10

Page 20

2	4	6	8	10
2	4	6	8	10
2	4	6	8	10

Page 21

2	4	6	8	10
2	4	6	8	10
2	4	6	8	10

Page 22

1	2	3	4	5	6	7	8
2	4	2	4	2	4	2	4
1	2	1	2	1	2	1	2
7	8	7	8	7	8	7	8
1	3	5	1	3	5	1	3

Page 23

red circle
blue square
blue rounded square
yellow triangle

Page 24

1	2	3	4	5	6	7
0	1	2	3	4	5	6
4	5	6	7	8	9	10

7	8	9	0	1	2
4	5	6	8	9	10

1	2	3	6	7	8
0	1	2	3	4	5

2	4	6	8	10

Page 25

5 bananas	2 potatoes	4 lemons
0 apples	1 container of milk	2 loaves of bread
blue square		

Page 26

3; 5; 4; 2; 6

Page 27

5; 4; 6; 4

Page 30

$1 + 3 = 4$ $3 + 3 = 6$ $4 + 1 = 5$ $2 + 4 = 6$ $2 + 1 = 3$

Page 31

$2 + 3 = 5$ $1 + 5 = 6$ $4 + 0 = 4$ $2 + 1 = 3$ $2 + 4 = 6$

Page 32

$3 + 2 = 5$ $1 + 1 = 2$
$6 + 0 = 6$ $5 + 1 = 6$
$2 + 5 = 7$ $4 + 3 = 7$

Page 33

$2 + 4 = 6$ $3 + 1 = 4$
$1 + 1 = 2$ $4 + 2 = 6$
$5 + 0 = 5$ $2 + 1 = 3$

Page 34

8, 10, 9, 7, 10

Page 35

$5 + 2 = 7$ $3 + 6 = 9$ $4 + 1 = 5$ $6 + 4 = 10$ $5 + 3 = 8$

Page 37

$4 + 6 = 10$; $7 + 3 = 10$; $1 + 9 = 10$; $2 + 8 = 10$; $5 + 5 = 10$

Page 38

$1 + 0 = 1$ $0 + 2 = 2$
$0 + 3 = 3$ $4 + 0 = 4$
$5 + 0 = 5$ $0 + 6 = 6$
$7 + 0 = 7$ $0 + 8 = 8$
$9 + 0 = 9$ $10 + 0 = 10$

Page 39

$1 + 1 = 2$; $2 + 2 = 4$; $3 + 3 = 6$;
$4 + 4 = 8$; $5 + 5 = 10$

Page 40

10	6	
2	5	
9	8	
10	5	
7	10	
9	8	7
7	4	

Page 41

$5 + 3 = 8$
$6 + 2 = 8$
$4 + 0 = 4$
$3 + 7 = 10$

Page 42

5, 4, 3, 2, 1, 0

Page 43

6, 5, 4, 3, 2, 1, 0

Page 44

6, 5, 4, 3, 2, 1, 0

Page 45

$3 - 0 = 3$
$5 - 0 = 5$
$9 - 0 = 9$
$4 - 0 = 4$
$10 - 0 = 10$
$2 - 0 = 2$
$7 - 0 = 7$

Page 46

4, 5, 3, 0, 1

Page 47

1, 3, 0, 6, 4

Page 48

7, 6, 5, 4, 3, 2, 1, 0

Page 49

8, 7, 6, 5, 4, 3, 2, 1, 0

Page 50

9	8
3	4
5	0
1	6

Page 51

4, 1, 3, 6, 0, 7, 2

Page 52

1 + 2 = 3	3 + 1 = 4
2 + 1 = 3	1 + 3 = 4
3 − 2 = 1	4 − 3 = 1
3 − 1 = 2	4 − 1 = 3
4 + 1 = 5	3 + 2 = 5
1 + 4 = 5	2 + 3 = 5
5 − 4 = 1	5 − 3 = 2
5 − 1 = 4	5 − 2 = 3

Page 53

4 + 2 = 6	5 + 2 = 7
2 + 4 = 6	2 + 5 = 7
6 − 4 = 2	7 − 5 = 2
6 − 2 = 4	7 − 2 = 5
4 + 3 = 7	5 + 3 = 8
3 + 4 = 7	3 + 5 = 8
7 − 4 = 3	8 − 5 = 3
7 − 3 = 4	8 − 3 = 5

Page 54

3	3	
3	8	
2	1	
1	4	5
5	7	4
5 + 3 = 8	6 + 4 = 10	
3 + 5 = 8	4 + 6 = 10	
8 − 5 = 3	10 − 6 = 4	
8 − 3 = 5	10 − 4 = 6	

Page 55

6 + 2 = 8	2 + 6 = 8	8 − 6 = 2	8 − 2 = 6
5 + 4 = 9	4 + 5 = 9	9 − 5 = 4	9 − 4 = 5
3 + 2 = 5	2 + 3 = 5	5 − 2 = 3	5 − 3 = 2
7 + 3 = 10	3 + 7 = 10	10 − 7 = 3	10 − 3 = 7

Page 56

10	11
12	13
14	15
16	17
18	19

Page 57

10 + 4 = 14	10 + 0 = 10
10 + 9 = 19	10 + 3 = 13
10 + 5 = 15	10 + 7 = 17
10 + 1 = 11	10 + 8 = 18

Page 58

10	20
30	40
50	60
70	80
90	100

Page 59

60	30
10	90
100	20
50	80
70	40

Page 60

Tens	Ones	
1	6	= 16
1	9	= 19
2	0	= 20
1	2	= 12
1	3	= 13
1	7	= 17
1	5	= 15
1	4	= 14

Page 61

Tens	Ones	
2	3	= 23
2	7	= 27
3	0	= 30
2	5	= 25
2	1	= 21
2	8	= 28
2	4	= 24
2	2	= 22

Page 62

Tens	Ones		Tens	Ones	
3	2	= 32	4	0	= 40
3	8	= 38	3	1	= 31
3	6	= 36	3	3	= 33
3	4	= 34	3	7	= 37
3	9	= 39	3	5	= 35

Page 63

Tens	Ones		Tens	Ones	
4	8	= 48	4	2	= 42
4	5	= 45	5	0	= 50
4	1	= 41	4	7	= 47
4	9	= 49	4	3	= 43
4	4	= 44	4	6	= 46

Page 64

Tens	Ones
1	3
2	8
3	5
4	7
5	4

Page 65

Tens	Ones
1	9
2	2
3	6
4	7
2	8

Page 66

Guess	Check
30 or 40	32
40 or 50	46
20 or 30	29

Page 67

Guess	Check
40 or 50	45
20 or 30	27
30 or 40	33

Page 68

Tens	Ones		Tens	Ones	
7	3	= 73	10	0	= 100
5	6	= 56	8	4	= 84
9	2	= 92	6	9	= 69
7	1	= 71	5	3	= 53
8	5	= 85	9	9	= 99

Page 69

Tens	Ones		Tens	Ones	
5	2	= 52	8	1	= 81
7	8	= 78	9	4	= 94
5	8	= 58	6	5	= 65
7	7	= 77			
8	9	= 89			

Page 70

42	43	44	45	35	36	37	38
86	87	88	89	70	71	72	73
19	20	21	22				

Page 71

63	64	65		28	29	30
16	17	18		81	82	83
37	38	39		70	71	72
46	47	48		94	95	96
68	69	70		55	56	57

Page 72

<	>
>	>
<	>
<	>

Page 73

=	<
>	<
<	=
>	>

Page 74

about 20	about 10
about 10	about 40

Page 75

12	about 10
18	about 20
63	about 60
84	about 80
39	about 40
97	about 100

Page 76

10 + 3 = 13	10 + 5 = 15
80 + 10 = 90	50 + 10 = 60
40	70

Tens	Ones		Tens	Ones	
3	6	= 36	8	2	= 82
6	0	= 60	9	5	= 95

<	<
=	>

91	92	93	94	95	96	97	98	99	100

Page 77

Guess	Check
30 or 40	27
40 or 50	43
about 20	17

Page 78

4¢, 9¢, 8¢, 18¢

Page 80

6¢, 9¢, 10¢, 18¢, 15¢

Page 81

9¢ matches the third set of coins.

12¢ matches the second set of coins.

6¢ matches the first set of coins.

17¢ matches the last set of coins.

10¢ matches the fourth set of coins.

Page 82

11¢, 14¢, 20¢, 22¢, 30¢

Page 83

40¢ matches the second set of coins.

17¢ matches the first set of coins.

10¢ matches the third set of coins.

25¢ matches the last set of coins.

21¢ matches the fourth set of coins.

Page 84

16¢, 15¢, 19¢, 20¢, 22¢

Page 85

46¢ matches the second set of coins.

35¢ matches the third set of coins.

23¢ matches the fourth set of coins.

36¢ matches the first set of coins.

31¢ matches the last set of coins.

Page 86

1 nickel matches 5 pennies.

1 dime and 1 penny match 6 pennies and 1 nickel.

1 dime matches 2 nickels.

1 nickel and 1 penny match 6 pennies.

2 dimes match 4 nickels.

1 dime and 5 pennies match 1 dime and 1 nickel.

Page 87

6¢	13¢
13¢	6¢
22¢	17¢
17¢	22¢
7¢	7¢

Page 88

Possible answers are given.

13¢: Circle 1 dime and 3 pennies.

14¢: Circle 1 dime and 4 pennies.

20¢: Circle 2 dimes.

35¢: Circle 3 dimes and 1 nickel.

Page 89

Possible answers are given.

30¢: Circle 3 dimes.

31¢: Circle 3 dimes and 1 penny.

6¢: Circle 1 nickel and 1 penny.

22¢: Circle 2 dimes and 2 pennies.

40¢: Circle 4 dimes.

Page 90

Possible answers are given.

2 dimes, 1 nickel

1 nickel, 1 penny

1 nickel

1 nickel, 1 penny

2 dimes, 1 nickel, 1 penny

Page 91

Possible answers are given.

2 pennies

1 nickel, 1 penny

2 dimes

1 dime, 1 nickel

1 dime, 1 penny

Page 92 Unit 5 Review

7¢, 18¢, 14¢, 26¢

11¢	17¢
17¢	11¢

Page 93

Possible answers are given.

Students should draw the coins needed.

3 dimes

1 dime, 2 pennies

1 penny

2 pennies

Page 94

Page 95

5; 12	7; 12
11; 12	2; 12
6; 12	9; 12
12; 12	1; 12

Page 96

11:00; 11	4:00; 4	9:00; 9
3:00; 3	8:00; 8	5:00; 5
7:00; 7	12:00; 12	1:00; 1

Page 97

7:00	11:00
1:00	8:00
3:00	10:00
5:00	9:00

Page 98 Students should draw the hands on the clocks to show each time.

3:00	5:00
1:00	7:00
2:00	9:00
12:00	10:00

Page 100

2; 3; 6
10; 11; 6
8; 9; 6
4; 5; 6
12; 1; 6

Page 102

7:30	11:30
12:30	8:30
3:30	10:30
4:30	9:30

Page 104

3:00	11:30
2:30	9:00
4:30	11:00
1:00	5:30

Page 106

1:00; 1	7:00; 7	9:00; 9
10:00; 10	4:00; 4	2:00; 2
12:30	2:30	8:30

Page 108

cube, prism, pyramid, sphere, cone, cylinder

Page 109

prism—flower box

sphere—globe

cube—cardboard box

cone—traffic cone

pyramid—Egyptian pyramid

cylinder—can

Page 111

rectangle	triangle	square
circle	square	triangle
circle	rectangle	circle

Page 114

4	4
3	3
4	4
0	0
3	3
4	4

Page 116

4, 6, 3

Page 118

4 in., 5 in., 1 in., 2 in.

Page 120

10 cm, 13 cm, 4 cm, 6 cm

Page 122 Guesses may vary.

4 in., 2 in., 5 in., 3 in.

Page 124

spheres, cones, cylinders

12 cm   4 in.

Page 99

Students should draw the hands on the clocks to show each time.

5:00, 10:00, 1:00, 11:00

Page 101

1;	2; 6
6;	7; 6
11;	12; 6
3;	4; 6
9;	10; 6

Page 103

5:30 matches the second clock.

6:30 matches the third clock.

12:30 matches the last clock.

9:30 matches the first clock.

Page 105

4:30	10:00
3:00	7:30
8:00	12:30

Page 107

11:00
4:30
1:00
10:00
8:30

Page 110

triangle, circle, square, rectangle, triangle

Page 115

yes	yes	no
yes	yes	no
yes	yes	no
no	no	yes
no	yes	yes
no	yes	yes

Page 117

5, 4, 6

Page 119

6 in., 3 in., 4 in., 5 in.

Page 121

15 cm, 7 cm, 10 cm, 15 cm

Page 123 Guesses may vary.

10 cm, 5 cm, 13 cm, 8 cm

Page 125

Guesses may vary.

3 in., 6 in., 2 in.